NEW HOPE FOR THE ARTHRITIC

- Explains Dr. Dong's treatment, the theories behind it, and the reason it works

- Includes documented case histories

- Discusses the importance of proper nutrition, how arthritis can be induced by chemicals in our food, the relation of arthritis to food allergy

- Examines the problem and manner of exercise for the arthritic

- Offers a complete guide to Dr. Dong's famous diet that includes:

> planning and buying advice
> cooking tips
> substitute suggestions
> a one-month menu plan
> dozens of sumptuous recipes

AND MORE!

Dr. Dong, in his new approach to the problem of arthritis, has pointed the way and his results are obvious. His book will give new hope to the arthritic.

Also by Collin H. Dong, M.D. and Jane Banks:

THE ARTHRITIC'S COOKBOOK

Copyright © 1975 by Collin H. Dong and Jane Banks

Library of Congress Catalog Card Number: 75-16388
ISBN 0-345-32728-4

This edition published by arrangement with Thomas Y.
Crowell Company, New York.

Printed in Canada

First Ballantine Books Edition: November 1976
Seventeenth Printing: July 1993

NEW HOPE
for the
ARTHRITIC

Collin H. Dong, M.D.
and
Jane Banks

BALLANTINE BOOKS • NEW YORK

This book is dedicated to the following Dongs:
Ten-Song (Guiding Star) Dong, my father
Yuk-Gee (Jade Pearl) Dong, my mother
Mil-lie (Elegant Beauty) Dong, my wife

Acknowledgments

I would like to express my gratitude and thanks to the following persons:

To Jane Banks, my coauthor, who insisted that we simply must write a second book to answer the many inquiries prompted by the first book. Although my work as a physician and businessman kept me busy from 8 A.M. to 7 P.M. daily, I was sure that I could cut down on a few hours of sleep to write the book. Having been convinced that it was important to explain my theory, I agreed to write the text of the book and to have Mrs. Banks do the recipes.

To Cynthia Vartan, my editor at Thomas Y. Crowell Company, who sent back my first draft, saying that all it needed was organization. Her confidence that I could write the book gave me the impetus to continue working on it.

To Dr. S. I. Hayakawa, my friend, who read the first draft and gave me invaluable suggestions about organizing it.

To Galen, my son, who planned my 24-hour day so that I could find at least four hours a day to work on this book. He even gave me six hours on Wednesdays to play golf.

To Eileen and Colleen, my daughters, for their time, their research, and their work in taking dictation and in transcription and revision of my copy.

And last, but certainly not least, to Millie, my wife, who tolerated my changes in mood, temper, and ideas. She sat for over twelve months taking dictation on thousands of pages of paper and then taking dictation on the revisions of each page. Her talent and skill as an expert typist saw me through this ordeal. Her capacity for work, judgment, and organization were intrinsic to the completion of this book. But most of all, for her love and affection.

Contents

Contents

NEW HOPE
for the
ARTHRITIC

Introduction

This book is based, first of all, on my own experience as one who recovered from a severe form of arthritis. It is further based in thirty-seven years of using my own dietary therapy on my patients who were suffering from the same or similar ailments. It is not a scientific work, in the sense of being based on thorough and well-authenticated scientific research.

What worked for me has achieved remarkable results for thousands of my patients. Many, in turn, referred others to me who suffered from arthritis—and they, too, found relief from their pains after following my regimen.

I would have started shouting from the housetops that I had made a great medical discovery, except for the following facts. First, when I made the initial discovery of my method, I was a young physician who was by no means ready to challenge medical orthodoxy. Second, I felt that I needed more experience.

The orthodox view on the subject of arthritis is dogmatic—and who was I to question the distinguished group of organized physicians who constitute the Arthritis Foundation? In a booklet entitled *Arthritis— the Basic Facts,* they said:

"People insist on believing that special diets or exotic foods are helpful in arthritis.

"The possible relationship of diet and arthritis has been thoroughly and scientifically studied.

"The simple proven fact is: no food has anything to do with causing arthritis and no food is effective in treating or 'curing' it.

"The proper diet for someone with arthritis is a normal, well-balanced, nourishing diet—the same things people without arthritis should eat."

Those are pretty intimidating words! Here I was, beginning to believe, because of my own experience, that there *was* a connection between diet and arthritis. But, there was the learned foundation announcing, as if with the voice of Jehovah: *"The relationship between diet and arthritis has been thoroughly and scientifically studied. The simple proven fact is: no food has anything to do with causing arthritis and no food is effective in treating or 'curing' it."*

Those words are formidable and final. Yet I could not accept their finality.

What is the state of the medical art so far as arthritis is concerned? Medical scientists all over the world—biochemists, immunologists, researchers conducting experiments on animals, others using sophisticated modern instruments of analysis—are trying to find, without success, the cause and cure of this dreaded disease.

Fifty million people in the United States suffer from arthritis at one or another level of severity—so the reader certainly either has it himself or is related to someone who has. Arthritis afflicts children as well as centenarians. And all those afflicted are in pain; $400 million annually is spent for ineffective "cures" and over-the-counter painkillers.

The orthodox treatment is large doses of aspirin. Proprietary drugs, developed as substitutes for aspirin, are also used—and some are selling like hotcakes. But all these drugs treat only symptoms, not the disease.

Consequently, once a diagnosis of arthritis is made, most patients are told in effect: "There is no cure for your ailment. You will simply have to live with it." They face years of recurrent, persistent, irritating pain and disability—wishing desperately for something, anything, to do about it!

When I was thirty-five years old, only seven years out of Stanford Medical School and my subsequent internship at San Francisco General Hospital, I was afflicted with arthritis. As it steadily became worse, with crippling pain in my joints, I also developed a severe generalized dermatitis.

I searched through my medical textbooks, through other books, and journals. I consulted my former professors and my medical colleagues. In three long years of progressive suffering, I found that there was nothing that physicians could do for me except prescribe large doses of aspirin—which was precisely what was giving me my skin disorder. I was genuinely at a dead end, doomed, as far as I could see, to unrelieved misery for the rest of my days.

When I recently told this story to my friend Dr. S. I. Hayakawa, the eminent semanticist and educator, he was reminded of a motto of his mentor, Count Alfred Korzybski, the founder of General Semantics, who said: "When things are really hopeless, that is where hope begins." In my preoccupation with acquiring a Western scientific education and becoming a physician in the Western sense, I had forgotten my background in Chinese culture. In my illness I became desperate enough to be thrown back to it. As I explain later in this book, I devised a simplified Chinese diet based on the simple food of my childhood—mainly fish, chicken, vegetables, and rice.

Two years ago my friend and former patient Mrs. Jane Banks and I collaborated in writing *The Arthritic's Cookbook,* a book of recipes using the foods allowed on my diet. Mrs. Banks, a talented cook and experienced hostess, had been a victim of severe and crippling arthritis.

Mrs. Banks and I received thousands of letters from readers all over the United States, Canada, and parts of Europe. Many of the letters substantiated my hypothesis. Many of them, moreover, stimulated further questions about the diet and about various aspects arthritis, and raised other inquiries which this book attempts to answer.

The present volume, then, has four purposes:

First, to give more information on rheumatic diseases so that the patient will have a clearer understanding of the illness, its course, and its nature—making it possible for him to cooperate with his own physician.

Second, to give an explanation of my dietary regimen, not only for arthritis sufferers but also for my medical colleagues, so that they may use it as an auxiliary treatment for their rheumatic disease patients. Since the diet is intended as an adjunctive treatment, the arthritis victim can start on the diet plan at any time.

Third, to give more elaborate menus to make it easier to maintain the diet for longer periods of time, and to facilitate daily cooking and meal preparation, by providing more recipes and cooking tips.

Finally, it is Mrs. Banks's hope, and mine, that the reader may enjoy, with the help of this book, freedom from pain, and therefore a healthier, happier, and longer life.

Several of my medical colleagues, knowing that I was working on this second book, sent statements expressly for publication endorsing my dietary precepts. I have chosen to include two of them here. The first is from Dr. Ione E. Railton, who has been associate clinical professor of medicine at the University of California Medical School since 1947.

"I believe that excellent results really need a commendation. My sister, Varian, whom Dr. Dong has treated for the past year, has had such a remarkable turn-about in her health status. She had an acute onset of rheumatoid arthritis at the age of fifty-five. The pain in her sternum and ribs was like angina, and we thought it was, until she was certain that it was related chiefly to the motions of deep breathing turning over in bed, and twisting. Next, her hips became painful and she had difficulties rising from chairs. Then, quite quickly came swollen, tender knees and ankles. She could barely walk and found the vibrations of car riding also caused pain. A rheumatologist put her on aspirin, cortisone and finally Indocin, which did help remarkably as long as she kept on a fairly high dosage regularly. She gained weight, her blood pressure became elevated and she was constantly fatigued and became desperately ill, to a point where she could not perform even the most menial task. She had heard of Dr. Dong's successful treatment of arthritis with a dietary program.

"So I arranged an appointment for her in March, 1972. She felt better after her second visit. Wisely Dr. Dong took her off her medications very slowly—two months, I recall, to taper down the cortisone. He put her on an elimination diet.

"I had interned under Dr. Albert Rowe, Sr., the eminent allergist, at the University of California, who published wheatless, milkless, eggless diets for hay fever, asthma, urticaria, and I reinforced the importance of diet to her. Besides, we come from an allergic family, both sides having pollen hay fever. She also exercised under warm water, slowly and to the point of relaxation, not muscle fatigue. I can state she was a faithful adherent to Dr. Dong's program and added to her diet only on his advice, not on mine, or her San Diego physician's. Every day she felt better. She lost 40 pounds, and naturally looked younger, took over more housekeeping duties, socialized with her two daughters and grandchildren. She even went on car rides, a bus trip, and this year, a trip to Canada.

"On our recent visit, she seemed entirely well except for easy fatiguability. No more ugly ankles, knee swellings and I think she could jitterbug with the same old zest—could she find one of us to keep up with her!

"In my clinic work, I've seen a lot of arthritis, rheumatoid and osteoarthritis. I was practicing when cortisone was discovered in 1949. We used it in 1950 with marvelous results. Patients got better almost at once, they threw away their crutches, and walked, the pain disappeared as well as did the swelling. We were all euphoric, patients and doctors; then came the side effects and our disillusionment: ulcers, h' pertension, diabetes and moon faces. We had to q' our generous doses, use it only for handling acute episodes and again rely on aspirin, physiotherapy, and supportive measures.

"Chronic diseases are always hard to handle, for they involve patients, family, employers, and social services. I knew the future for my sister better than she—that we were all being involved in her health adjustment. Emotional factors play an important role in rheumatoid arthritis, so we all tried to alleviate stress and anxiety. That is not easy in present everyday living. Now that we have a new approach to this problem which is geared to the total patient, his diet, his general health measures, exercise, acupuncture, I think rheumatoid arthritis will not be as devastating a problem as it was to all of us involved. But it takes interest on the part of the doctor in all facets of the disease and treatment, and a better-than-usual cooperation from the patient. That may mean frequent appointments, education, reassurance and modification of environment.

"Dr. Dong has pointed the way, and his results are obvious. His patients are working and walking again!"

The second statement is from Dr. John R. Upton, who graduated from the Stanford University School of Medicine in 1934. He was certified by the American Board of Obstetrics and Gynecology and was the former chief of obstetrics and gynecology at St. Luke's Hospital, San Francisco. Dr. Upton was also associate clinical professor at the University of California Hospital, San Francisco.

"As a doctor of medicine, I have always been aware of the importance of a proper diet, and its full value was dramatically demonstrated through my personal experience this year. I was the victim of an arthritic condition which was increasingly painful. I had received the maximum amount of cortisone deemed advisable, and to resort to pain-killing drugs for the rest of my life was repugnant to me. It was then that I sought the help of Dr. Collin Dong, who I knew to be most successful in the treatment of this affliction.

"I am only one of Dr. Dong's grateful patients who will be forever indebted to him for his excellent care.

To relieve my arthritic pains he outlined a plan which included a dietary regimen, moderate amounts of medication, and exercise. The elimination of the over-riding cause of the pain through a prescribed diet was a miracle.

"The delectable dietary regimen is fully outlined in Dr. Dong's and Jane Banks's first book, *The Arthritic's Cookbook*, and it is the diet that I myself successfully followed.

"A cookbook is many things to many people. It can be a simple primer to intitiate the aspiring novice. Again, it may present only the sophisticated dishes, tempting us by the richness of their sauces, the subtleties of their textures and flavor. For those who seek the exotic and unusual, there are books specializing in the cuisines of many lands, mysterious and foreign to our palate. Outranking all others is *The Arthritic's Cookbook*, which offers that treasure beyond measure, good health!

"Dr. Dong's second book, *New Hope for the Arthritic*, furnishes a fuller explanation of his theories, including some of his clinical case histories. He includes his dietary regimen, and discusses the elimination of the ingredients which upset the body chemistry, causing pain and malfunction, and resulting in physical incapacities. He also discusses proper nutrition.

"I hasten to point out that such a regiment does not deny one of the joys of good food. As those who follow the suggested regimen in his books will discover, it offers a vast choice of nature's finest produce prepared with an endless variety of flavors, textures, and seasonings.

"I recommend *New Hope for the Arthritic* to all who would find good fare, good health, and the good life."

I am deeply grateful to Dr. Railton and to Dr. Upton for their encouragement and support. It is good to know that their medical experience coincides so much with my own, especially on the question of the relation between diet, health, *and illness*.

But I must come back to the fact mentioned at the beginning—that this book is the result of experience, and not the result of thoroughly tested and validated scientific theories. Such results on the subject of diet and illness are still to come.

I myself am not a research scientist. I am a practicing physician, immersed in the daily aches and pains and discomforts of a varied collection of patients of every race and nationality, from every walk of life. To discover the biochemical facts about the relation of diet to rheumatic diseases requires rigorous and painstaking research of a kind that I have neither the training nor the time to perform.

It is my deepest hope, thereore, not only that sufferers from arthritis and rheumatic diseases will be helped by this book, but also that scientific investigators in this field will be stimulated by what I have written here to do more intensive research into the relationship between diet and arthritis.

1

Diet and Nutrition: An Important but Neglected Subject

Case History

NAME:	Mr. G.I.
RESIDENCE:	California
AGE:	43
OCCUPATION:	Manager of service bureau
DIAGNOSIS:	Polyarthritis
DURATION:	Five years
FIRST VISIT:	April 13, 1973
PREVIOUS MEDICATION:	Aspirin, Indocin, Butazolidin, Empirin compound with codeine, Darvon, corticosteroid
INTERVIEWED:	January 26, 1974

"The onset of my arthritis started about five years ago. It began in my right wrist, went down into my hip and also affected my sternum. My arthritis got worse and worse and I became more and more restricted and restrained. It was very frustrating to me.

"I went to several doctors and had different kinds of diagnoses. One doctor said it was early osteoarthritis. Another specialist said it was polyarthritis. They gave me various kinds of painkilling medicines, but did not help me at all. So I finally went to the Rheumatic and Arthritis Disease Clinic in my home town. I was treated there for a year and a half. I was going through test after test until I felt like a human guinea pig. Because of my pain, they started giving me five different prescription drugs. They also gave me cortisone orally and by injection, and other types of pain killers. All this was still doing me no good. You have no idea how desperate I began to get.

"As Administration Manager of a service bureau company, I had to do a lot of sitting, walking, and sometimes running, on the job. I had also been very active in my personal life. I was an active member of the Y.M.C.A. Youth Program. We hike, camp and have many sports activities. Since the onset of my sickness, I could hardly carry on my job, and I had to give up participation in the Y.M.C.A. for two years.

"I first saw Dr. Dong on April 13, 1973.

["Mr. G. I.'s experience is typical of the manner in which some physicians treat rheumatic disease cases. Large doses of medication such as aspirin, Indocin, Butazolidin, codeine, Darvon, steroids and other medication are prescribed in desperation because the patient does not respond to their therapy program. The fact that some patients might be allergic to any one of these drugs, thereby exacerbating the illness, is completely ignored.

When Mr. G. I. came to my office, I analysed the previous treatment and suspected that he could be allergic to one of the chemicals in the medication that had been prescribed. The patient was advised to discontinue the medication except for Darvon, codeine and steroids for pain. Mr. G. I. was given my usual lecture on the relation of nutrition to health and told to adhere strictly to the Dong Diet. He was given acupuncture treatments once a month.

On January 26, 1974, after eight months of treatment, the patient was practically rejuvenated. He had lost twenty-two pounds. His blood pressure, which was elevated before he came to my office, was normal. The patient no longer required any medication. His joint mobility was almost normal.]

"Now I am a new man. A lot of things happened to me. My pain was alleviated almost immediately. I began to sleep better at night, and the anxiety that I had about all my problems began to go away. That diet is really something. I feel, as the Spanish say, 'Muy macho.' I feel that I am not limited at all now, or restrained in any of my activities. I feel ten or fifteen years younger, I can participate in the family sports and it is great. You do not realize what pain is, or was, until you get rid of it. I went back to my Y.M.C.A. work and recently we went on a week-end overnight. We went on a fifteen mile hike down through the mountains and trails. I was able to climb like a young mountain goat."

The great physician Sir William Osler once said, "When I see an arthritic patient walk in the front door of my office, I want to walk out the back door." In my office in San Francisco I have no back door. When new arthritic patients come painfully in or are helped in by their relatives, I have to accept the challenge they present to me. Every one of these patients is, like Mr. G. I. whose case I have just cited, a chronic case who had been treated by several doctors and clinics with orthodox methods. My office is a "port of last resort."

During the past thirty years I have read most periodicals, medical journals, books, and scientific papers on rheumatic diseases. Whenever possible I attend clinical demonstrations and seminars throughout the world. My intense interest in the field is due not only to the fact that I have been the victim of arthritis myself, but also because I feel the need to try to alleviate the pains of others whenever possible.

My own treatment for the arithritic patients who come to me is principally a dietary therapy, based on my belief that the causes of rheumatic diseases are chemical poisoning from the additives and preservatives that are put into our foods and from allergy to certain foods. In subsequent chapters I will go into my reasons for this theory in detail. I will also discuss the types of arthritis, their treatment by orthodox methods and my own treatment, longevity and exercise as they relate to the arthritic, and acupuncture as an adjunct to my treatment of the disease. I want to begin, however, with the all-important but neglected topics of diet and nutrition and how they effect our health and well being, for an understanding of this is basic to everything else I will say.

Diet and nutrition are not the same thing. Diet refers to the food that people eat while nutrition refers to the assimilation of food into the bloodstream so that it can be used by the human body. Perhaps the clearest way to show how the food we eat alters our whole body chemistry is to give you first a brief refresher course on the process of digestion.

When a housewife shops in the supermarket for the family meal, she usually brings home three basic materials: meat (including fats), vegetables, and bread (carbohydrates). Most recipes are made from one or more of these three ingredients.

After you put the food into your mouth and start chewing it, digestion begins. The salivary gland enzymes begin changing the starch into maltose, and the food then passes down the esophagus to the stomach, which is a food reservoir. The gastric juices, consisting mainly of hydrochloric acid, start mixing with the food. These also activate another enzyme called pepsin, which starts the protein digestion. As more food comes down into the stomach from the esophagus, the gastric muscles contract and mix the food thoroughly with the digestive juices. Soon it becomes a thick gruel, and gradually this gruel works down into the duodenum, which comprises the first twelve inches of the small intestine. It takes about four hours for the average meal to go through the stomach into the duodenum. There, other secretions, bile from the liver and alkaline pancreatic juice from the pancreas, neutralize the acid gruel. The function of the bile is to produce an alkaline reaction in the intestines and the emulsification and absorption of fats.

Let me interrupt the digestive process here to give you a picture of your intestines. The whole intestinal tract is twenty-six feet long. First there is the one-foot-long duodenum. The next part is called the jejunum, which is eight feet long and about one and one-half inches in diameter. Then come the twelve feet of the slightly smaller ileum. The end of the ileum connects with the five-foot-long large intestine in the right lower abdomen near your appendix.

To a large degree, the upper intestines are free of microbes because stomach acid kills most of them. However, the lower intestines contain upwards of fifty varieties of bacteria, and there are billions of each in that area, which also help in the digestion of food.

Going back to the digestive process, at the time that the gruel reaches the duodenum, it causes the duodenum to produce a hormone called secretin. Secretin goes through the blood to stimulate the pancreas into instant secretion of its alkaline digestive juices. Then these pour into the duodenum, neutralizing the acids. The pancreatic juices also contain three principal enzymes that break up the protein, fats, and carbohydrates into basic building materials for the body. One of these chemicals is trypsin, which initiates the breakdown of proteins into amino acids. Another enzyme, amylase, converts starches into carbohydrates in the form of glucose, and a third, lipase, attacks the fat globules, breaking them into fatty acids and glycerin. As these nutrients pass through the twenty-one feet of small intestines, the processed meal is absorbed into the bloodstream by millions of villi, microscopic, fingerlike projections on the walls of the intestines. The function of the villi is of utmost importance. They separate the amino acids, glucose, and fats from the waste material. The fats are absorbed and sent through the lymphatic vessels and then into the bloodstream. The amino acids and glucose are absorbed through capillaries of the villi and then into the liver. The processing of a meal usually takes from three to eight hours. The rest of the watery gruel goes into the large intestine. There the water is taken back into the bloodstream. Waste matter, including fibers and cellulose, are passed from the body as fecal matter.

After the digested meal has been absorbed through the millions of villi into the bloodstream, it goes through the liver, which is the great detoxifier. This means that the liver has the ability to change poisonous substances into nonpoisonous chemicals. For instance, the steak that becomes amino acids in the intestines before it is absorbed into the bloodstream, cannot be used until the liver changes its character so that it is fit for human use, or else it would be poisonous. From the liver the processed meal goes with the returning bloodstream into the right side of the heart, then into the lungs, where the blood is refreshed by giving up carbon dioxide and absorbing oxygen. The refreshed blood with all its components is then returned to the left side of the heart, where it is pumped into the entire vascular system of 60,000 miles of blood vessels. The 60 trillion cells in the body of every human adult are supplied with oxygen and food by this process. (I will tell you more about this in the next chapter.)

All of the above discussion is a very sketchy description of of what happens to a meal. Actually the process is so complicated that scientists are constantly discovering new enzymes and hormones that aid in the digestive process. The functioning of the human body in its entirety is a mystery that may never be completely unraveled.

The groceries that were made into the evening meal have now been mixed with the chemicals of the blood to become part of the huge chemical plant in the body. There are millions of chemical reactions taking place every second of the day. In short, the foods that we consume give us energy and the basis of life. They perform this function through the mechanical and chemical actions of the digestive system and the trillions of cells in our body.

It should be fairly obvious by now that the quality and quantity of food that we eat can and do alter the whole body chemistry. The physiology of the body, the process of digestion, and man's biochemistry have not changed much since the time of Pleistocene man, who lived approximately five hundred thousand years ago. The present-day human being was formed by the diet of the first man. There have been no significant changes in the basic foodstuffs—meat, vegetables, and carbohydrates.

Today's inventions and industrialization have given us many spectacular timesaving conveniences. But when we include food processing as a mark of achievement, with its addition of tons of chemicals to color food, to enhance its taste, and to preserve it, we have ignored what these added substances do to our bodies. It is very likely that these added chemicals cause many of the physical and mental disorders in our society today.

A Trip to Fantasyland

I recently asked fifty people—lawyers, accountants, insurance brokers, bankers, and other nonmedical people—what is meant by the cellular structure of the human body. Not one of them knew. Becoming better acquainted with the marvelous structure of the human body and its functions is not only a source of intellectual delight and satisfaction, but it also gives one an approach to proper living. In order to make this discussion more meaningful and understandable, I'm going to take you on a short trip to Fantasyland.

I live in San Francisco on top of the famous and historic Telegraph Hill. The view from my apartment gives a panoramic scene of the two bridges and the beautiful bay. One day recently, redevelopment started at the foot of Telegraph Hill. Demolition began on a large seventy-five-year-old coldstorage building. Instead of using the conventional steel ball to knock down the walls of the building, teams of workmen began taking it down brick by brick, perhaps because old bricks are more valuable today than newly manufactured ones.

This unusually slow method of disassembling a structure in these days of speed somehow excited my imagination. That night in my dreams, I found myself walking into the huge brick building at the foot of the hill. When I entered, I discovered an amazing interior. Not only were the walls made of bricks of all shapes, sizes, and colors, but everything inside the building was also made of bricks. I ascended the stairway to the top floor where I saw a huge sculpture of a human head, complete in every detail—with brains, nerves, eyes, ears, nose, throat, mouth and neck. It was a beautiful mosaic—composed entirely of bricks. Walking down a spiral stairway built around the sculpture, I saw on the next floor an extension of this sculpture, a chest with lungs, heart, glands, and all the blood vessels. This also was made in the same strange way—with bricks.

The next floor contained more of the sculpture—a replica of the abdomen, with the diaphragm, duodenum, small intestines, large intestines, liver, pancreas, kidneys, and spleen. On the next floor were the reproductive organs of the female, the uterus, the tubes, the ovaries, and also the bladder. Down again to another floor, and there was the reproductive system of the male with the genital organs. From the second floor down to the basement, the sculpture was of the two legs and feet, showing the muscular and bone structure of the limbs. To my surprise, on closer examination, each one of these bricks was alive, and each was nourished by tiny vessels made of bricks.

Suddenly I was awakened by a telephone call. It was an unimportant call, but what was important was that I now had an idea of a novel way to present the human anatomy and physiology to my readers. For, to understand any medical subject, one must have some knowledge of the functions of the human body.

New Concepts of Microscopic Anatomy and Physiology

The human body in its entirety is made up of about 60 trillion bricks, or cells, just like the sculpture in my Fantasyland. From here on, I will refer to the body cells as bricks because I think this is more picturesque and I hope more understandable for the reader to envision.

The most wonderful process of life is the fertilization of the egg brick by the sperm brick in the female body. At that moment the fertilized germ brick is a human individual in a one-brick stage of development. This brick then splits into two bricks and divides over and over again until a baby is formed. This process is similar to the construction of a building. The first brick must be laid, then many other bricks must be added in order to complete the building.

Early in their development, the bricks all look alike. But when more and more bricks are being reproduced, some begin to take on special characteristics and look different from the others. This is called the differentiation stage. Thus we have groups called muscle bricks, skin bricks, nerve bricks, connective tissue bricks, and blood bricks.

Not only do they look different, they also have different purposes. The muscle bricks specialize in movement, the nerve bricks receive and transmit stimuli, epithelial bricks specialize in manufacturing secretions and skin, blood bricks specialize in transporting oxygen and nutrients to all the other trillions of bricks, and connective tissue bricks form many structures of the body and hold all the parts together.

Each and every brick carries on all the processes of life—they live and die, they take in food, they eliminate waste, they respond to stimuli, they move, and they reproduce other bricks of their own kind. Of all the wonderful skills that the body is capable of performing, the unsurpassed accomplishment is its capacity to reproduce its own kind and pass on genetic substances for future generations.

Millions of bricks die every second, and just as many new ones are born. Skin bricks reproduce every ten to twelve hours, while others, such as muscle and fat bricks, reproduce more slowly. Some bricks live longer than others. The only kinds that do not reproduce themselves are the brain bricks. Since you are supplied with more brain bricks than you will ever need in a lifetime, reproduction of these is not necessary. Also, nature seems to have made brain bricks stronger than most of the other trillions of bricks in the body because man's mental processes are still stable when many other groups of bricks are no longer functioning.

It is important to realize that each group of bricks in the human body is related to every other. They somehow communicate with each other, possibly through enzymes or hormones as well as through the nervous system.

When a person thinks, not only are the brain bricks used, but all the bricks in the body play some part in the thinking process. The muscle, the gland, and the blood bricks, and even the bricks in the digestive system all team together as a unit to help in the function of thinking. If you walk, you do not walk with your legs alone; the brain bricks start out by giving you an idea, and all the other bricks in the whole system help you to arrive at your destination. Many other emotions, too, such as fear, hunger, and other bodily states, require the action of the whole organism.

Amazing New View of Bricks (Cells)

Recent basic research has brought to light a new concept of the functions of the 60 trillion bricks of our body. Very few people, including scientists, know that bricks have appetites and special diets. When I studied medicine, and up to a short time ago, the bricks of our body were considered just a sack of fluid with chemicals and genetic substances. Research has given the bricks new intricate dimensions that I referred to. They live and die, they take in foods, they eliminate waste, they respond to stimuli, they move and reproduce bricks of their own kind. With this knowledge the exciting headlines concerning cancer in the newspapers should not be a mystery to you.

A Nobel prize-winning scientist, Dr. Christian de Duve, professor of medicine at Rockefeller University, suggested studying the diets of cancer cells, then slipping potent anticancer drugs into the food they liked best, as a new way of killing them.

Of course, this book does not deal with cancer, although I mention it several times, and in order to explain this theory, it is enough to think of cancer cells as *criminals* in our orderly society. They are bricks that do not conform to orderly multiplications, they start multiplying without inhibition, thus causing growth, such as tumors. Tumors, because of their constant growth, cause neighboring bricks to be crowded and injured, leading to malfunction. The cancer bricks can also spread through the bloodstream, causing tumors elsewhere in our body.

"Some cells in the human body are very avid eaters, others are less greedy. What is needed now," says Dr. De Duve, "is a detailed inventory of the tastes of cells, and their favorite foodstuff."

Dr. de Duve and his group in Europe and the United States have been tying powerful anticancer drugs to a carrier. The goal would be to kill the cancer bricks without harming the good ones, should the appetites of the cancer bricks be found to be different. One need only think of putting poison on cheese for rats. This ties in quite well with my new concept of histology and physiology, and is the reason that I introduced, at this point, the subject of cancer, which vitally concerns everyone.

Why Does a Person Get Sick?

How does all this relate to diet, nutrition, health, and well-being? Well, let's continue with the digestive process and see what happens to the nutrients. When they reach the heart, the trillions of heart bricks contract and pump them through its 60,000 miles of vascular system to all parts of the body. The heart with its vascular system can be compared to a water-pipe system in a large building.

Each group of bricks has different functions, and therefore will require different types of nutrients. One group may want certain minerals, others may want some vitamins, glucose, and amino acids, and still others may want hormones. It all depends on the needs of each brick or group of bricks.

Now, let me give you a typical example of why someone gets sick. If before an evening meal John Jones drinks three or more cocktails, what happens to the trillions of bricks that make up his body?

The cocktail goes through the digestive system from the mouth to the stomach and into the intestines, where it is changed into ethyl alcohol. This chemical is then absorbed through the villi into the bloodstream. From here it goes into the liver, where it is detoxified into harmless carbon dioxide and water. The capacity of the liver to detoxify alcohol is about one-half a cocktail or one glass of wine per hour. If more than this amount is forced into the liver, its capacity is overburdened. The toxic alcohol overflows and is then transported to the heart, whence it is pumped throughout John Jones's body. All the trillions of bricks are more or less poisoned, but the brain bricks seem to have an affinity for alcohol. As a result, it concentrates more in that area. Then our Mr. Jones is sick! He cannot articulate clearly, he loses his equilibrium because his muscle bricks are poisoned, and he is emotionally upset because his nerve bricks are also toxic.

If John Jones continues this behavior over a period of years, a large number of his liver bricks will be destroyed, and he will have a disease known as cirrhosis of the liver. His kidney bricks are also affected, resulting in nephritis. If John Jones's heart bricks are also injured, chronic myocarditis and cardiac decompensation will develop. Other parts of the body are affected in the same manner, and if enough of these trillions of bricks are weakened and destroyed, death occurs.

This sequence of events, caused by alcohol, is duplicated when the body takes in other poisonous substances, such as chemical additives in foods and microbial agents (bacteria and viruses).

Diseases Caused by Dietary Indiscretion

Although the purpose of food is to maintain and sustain life by giving the body necessary nutrition, dietary indiscretion has been practiced by all affluent nations from time immemorial. Food is utilized not only as a symbol of wealth but also for social intercourse. Even today in our advanced, intelligent, scientific world, food is used in the same imprudent and uninhibited manner of the Roman Empire before its downfall. Sybaritic living is one of the great human failings.

The inhuman routine of "a good breakfast," coffee breaks, an "adequate" lunch, snacks, cocktails, gourmet dinners, and constant nibbling while watching television has created a desperate medical problem in this land of abundance. One-fourth of our food goes into nourishment, and three-fourths goes into making us ill.

Scientific studies over the past three decades have definitely shown that what we eat can cause such degenerative diseases as heart disease, strokes, diabetes, and hypertension. A degenerative disease, according to *Dorland's Medical Dictionary*, ". . . occurs when there is a chemical change of the tissue from a normal to a less functionally active form." These disorders account for 70 percent of the annual death rate in the United States, a number that is growing at an ever-increasing rate.

Government reports indicate that in 1974 over 1 million people died of heart and vascular diseases, and approximately 20 million people have diabetes, 26 million are suffering from hypertension, 10 million suffer from asthma, and 1 million have gout.

These figures have evoked the concern of the federal government, and recently a national conference was called by the United States Committee on Nutrition and Human Needs, where every aspect of nutrition in relation to diseases was debated, discussed,

and pondered. The conclusion of this conference was
startling:

"We are a nation of nutritional illiterates. A large
part of the population takes its opinion about nutrition
from advertising, much of that being misinformation,
appealing to the eye and taste rather than a sense of
nutritional value. Many of our serious diseases can be
attributed to this dietary ignorance."

The American Well-Balanced Diet

Why are we labeled in such derogatory terms as
"nutritional illiterates"? What sort of diet are we
Americans eating now? What sort of diet do the medical and nutritional authorities recommend? Let's see
what the widely taught well-balanced diet means.
Since this book is mainly concerned with rheumatic
diseases, here is what is recommended in the Arthritis
Foundation's booklet, *Diet and Arthritis:*

"All the foods any arthritic needs can be found in
local food markets—but there is overwhelming evidence that nutritionally balanced meals eaten regularly benefit anyone's overall health, muscle tone, and
in the case of arthritis, build ability to resist the wear
and tear of the disease. Although some minor adjustments in specific items may be required, in general the
good diet for anyone, whether you have arthritis or
not, is based on selection from four food groups.
Briefly, they are the milk group; the meat group; the
vegetable and fruit group; and the bread and cereal
group. (1) The milk group: use two or more cups of
milk, or its equivalent daily; (2) the meat group: use
two or more servings daily; (3) the vegetable and fruit
group: use at least four servings of vegetables and
fruits daily; (4) the bread and cereal group: use four
or more servings daily."

If the above advice is beneficial, then every citizen
in the nation should have relatively good health. Why,
then, the continuous increase in so many chronic and
degenerative diseases that are not caused by germs or
viruses? And, if the so-called well-balanced American

diet is the main factor leading to such degenerative diseases as heart trouble, hypertension, strokes, diabetes, and even cancer, doesn't it seem logical that improper diet may lead to another degenerative disease, namely, arthritis?

Not to those in the Arthritis Foundation. Other researchers hint at nutrition's relationship to arthritis, but perhaps because of timidity they are reluctant to encroach upon the preserves of the foundation, which specifically pronounces:

"The relationship between diet and arthritis has been thoroughly and scientifically studied. The simple proven fact is: no food has anything to do with causing arthritis and no food is effective in treating or 'curing' it."

Let's look more closely at some specific items in this well-balanced diet and see what scientists have discovered.

Milk and Dairy Products

The Federal Trade Commission is bringing the California Milk Producers' Advisory Board to task for the milk advertising all over the nation. The commission's complaint challenges those familiar claims that: "Everybody needs milk," and "Milk has something for everybody," and states that for some people milk might be downright harmful.

In the March 11, 1975, issue of the *National Enquirer,* Dr. Kurt A. Oster, chief of cardiology at Park City Hospital, Bridgeport, Connecticut, said: "Homogenized milk is one of the major causes of heart diseases in the United States. The fat in the milk contains a substance called xanthine oxidase, or XO, an enzyme. This enzyme will attack the heart and its arteries if it enters the bloodstream; and it is able to get into the bloodstream from homogenized milk.

"When old-fashioned, non-homogenized milk is drunk, the body excretes the XO like any other waste. But when milk is homogenized, the breakup of the fat allows the tiny particles of XO to go through the walls of the intestine into the bloodstream and reach the heart and artery tissues.

"The XO acts chemically to scar the artery walls and heart tissue. The body tries to repair the damage by raising the cholesterol level of the blood, and depositing protective fatty material on the scars. If the process continues, the fatty material begins to clog the arteries, causing heart disease.

"Homogenized milk is the main reason why the United States' cardiac death rate is the highest in the world, next to Finland's."

Dr. Kurt Esselbacher, chairman of the Department of Medicine of the Harvard Medical School, said: "I am in full support of Dr. Oster's overall concept. Homogenized milk, because of its XO content, is one of the major causes of heart disease in the United States."

Dr. Oster further claimed: "The foundations of heart trouble start early in most Americans, because children drink so much milk. The damage caused by XO is a long-term process. The XO builds up in the body. The first 10 to 15 years, when most children drink a lot of milk—that's when the real damage is done."

The results of autopsies performed during the Korean and Vietnam wars on deceased soldiers substantiated the above statement. Several hundred autopsies were performed, and in one-half of the cases, a heart disease called atherosclerosis was found in the coronary arteries. These young men ranged in age from nineteen to thirty.

At a recent meeting of the American Public Health Association, Dr. George Christakis, formerly nutritional chief of New York's Mount Sinai School of Medicine, stated: "Forcing an infant to empty his bottle of cow's milk, and allowing a youngster to join in the McDonald generation, fueled by hamburgers, malted milk, and French fries, can set the stage for chronic diseases in later life. One third of all American men between the ages of twenty and fifty have high cholesterol levels and are high-risk heart attack possibilities.

"Cow's milk is ideal for calves. It has three times the protein of human milk, but it is not as digestible for a human. It is high in saturated fat, not absorbed as well by the human infant. It is not the perfect food for humans. It was designed for the calf which doubles its weight in fifty days, while the human does this in one hundred and fifty days. . . . Making the nation nutritionally aware means changing the American way of eating at every level."

Dr. Douglas H. Sandberg, associate professor of pediatrics at the University of Miami School of Medicine, said: "Milk isn't well tolerated by large segments of the world population. This is particularly true of the nonwhite majority. Some studies show that as many as 70% of the blacks do not digest it properly. In spite of this information, milk continues to be a major food in school free-lunch programs. Many Negro children who participate in these programs get enough lactose a day to cause them to have such symptoms as abdominal pain and diarrhea." Dr. Sandberg recommended that if such symptoms were found to be prevalent in black children drinking milk, it should be eliminated from school lunches and another protein source substituted.

Saturated Fats

Dr. Paul Leren, professor of medicine at Oslo University, has produced convincing evidence that a change in diet can prevent heart disease. He had a group of 412 middle-aged men (from the ages of forty-four to sixty-four), who had a history of one previous heart attack. The question to be answered was: Can a second heart attack be prevented if the patient eliminates animal fats from his diet?

Dr. Leren divided these patients into two groups: 206 of his subjects were put on a diet that contained no cream, whole milk, butter, fatty meats, such as beef, lamb, or pork, or egg yolks—almost the Dong Diet. These people were not given any sort of medication. The other 206 subjects continued to eat what they'd always eaten.

Dr. Leren followed these people for five years, and at the end of the period, the score stood like this: Among the 206 dieters there were 43 heart attacks in all. Among the 206 nondieters, there were 64 heart attacks in the group, 21 more than among the other patients. Ten of the dieters died; 23 of the nondieters died. In summary, a diet relatively free of animal fats can prevent corornary heart attacks.

Dr. Jeremiah Stamler, an eminent heart researcher from Chicago, while participating in the American Congress of Cardiology, said: "The opulent, high-fat, heavy-smoking life of the American may be a far more widespread cause of death from heart disease than race, genetics, or even high blood pressure." Dr. Stamler feels the problem is the way that we define the "good life—our well-marbled steaks, our whipped cream and buttery cakes, and cigarettes."

The American Heart Association, after analyzing data and the results of experiments with the so-called well-balanced American diet over the past two decades, has seen its detrimental effects. The association published a cookbook to counteract the misconception underlying the American way of eating. On the jacket of this book is the astute remark: "The reason for being, and your reason for using it—are as basic as the most basic recipe in its pages. More than a million Americans die annually from heart and circulatory problems. The foods that we eat, especially fatty foods, are one of the risk factors in heart disease. Our diet is one factor we can do something about."

The American Heart Association's low-fat, low-cholesterol diet is also approved by the Food and Nutrition Board of the National Academy of Sciences—National Research Council and the Council on Foods and Nutrition of the American Medical Association, which also recommended it in a joint statement in July, 1972.

Diet is now suspected as being the cause of certain types of cancer. The *Wall Street Journal* of October 25, 1973, stated: "The affluent American diet, already indicted as the major factor in heart disease, now is being linked to another mortal ailment—cancer of the colon and rectum."

There is little doubt that our diet is somehow related to the risk of getting colon-rectal cancer. In recent weeks one study has put the spotlight on beef. Other research is indicating fat. One theory pinpoints refined flour and the lack of roughage.

At the moment, the linking of colon-rectal cancer with the diet is largely statistical. For some time, researchers have been mystified by the fact that there are definite geographical differences in death rates from this form of cancer. Since cancer occurs in the bowel, the scientists' first attempts to explain these geographical differences have focused on the dietary differences between the countries.

The results strongly indicate that the researchers are on the right track. For instance, among the Japanese who migrated to Hawaii in 1920 and 1930 and are now in the age groups where colon-rectal cancer is the most common, it was found that the colon-cancer rate is much higher than the rate in Japan, though not as high as the overall United States rate.

A study was made to see if the rate among the Hawaiian Japanese had anything to do with their switching away from the traditional Japanese diet of vegetables and fish to the meat-heavy, fat-heavy American diet. Drs. William Haenszel, John W. Berg, and others at the National Cancer Institute, found that the Japanese immigrants who developed the malignancy had a history of eating considerably more beef than did their fellow immigrants who did not develop the disease.

Dr. Berg said: "There is now substantial evidence that beef consumption is a key factor in determining bowel cancer incidence."

Another frequent cause of death on the American scene is "strokes." A stroke is caused by a blockage of the arteries leading to the brain. Dr. John S. la Due of the Sloan-Kettering Institute for Cancer Research in New York City, explaining how this happens, warned against diets rich in saturated fats because such foods interfere with the machinery inside blood vessels that is designed to dissolve blood clots.

Sugar

Some of the most serious diseases are caused by too much sugar consumption. Our annual consumption of sugar per capita is over one hundred pounds. Americans spent approximately $2.5 billion on candy in 1974, and now that sugar prices are so inflated, this sum could possibly rise to $7 billion in 1975. Further statistics show that each year the average American consumes about 20 pounds of ice cream and 25 gallons of soft drinks—and that soft-drink consumption is increasing by 10 percent each year. This habit has caused three of the most common diseases in the United States—dental caries, or decay, which costs billions of dollars for dental health care annually; diabetes, which afflicts millions of Americans; and obesity, the embarrassing and detrimental disease that is now the scourge of Western society.

Alcohol

Another disease on the upsurge, that is due to luxurious living, is liver disease, caused by the excessive use of alcohol. Figures show that 40 gallons of beer, wine, and liquor were imbibed per capita in the United States in 1974. This total is rising by about 10 percent annually.

Inadequate sexual performance in men has even been linked to excessive use of alcohol, according to an article in the Chicago *Tribune*.

"Infertility, impotence, and feminine characteristics were found in nearly all 37 men with alcoholic liver disease in a new study conducted at Boston City Hospital.

"The latest findings blame alcohol-induced damage to two sex-controlling glands at the base of the brain.

"The glands—the pituitary and the hypothalamus —produce hormones called IH and PH. These enable the testicles to manufacture sperm and testosterone (the male sex hormone.)

"Sixty-eight percent of the men in the study, age 29 to 65, had markedly reduced levels of testosterone. All had decreased sperm levels, and only one man had normal seminal fluid."

Pervasiveness of Chemical Additives

Because we Americans are always in a hurry for everything, the processed-food industry has, in the last fifteen years, grown to be one of the giant enterprises in the United States. There are over 30,000 different kinds of foodstuffs in our supermarkets, grossing about $130 billion a year. Manufactured and processed packaged-food items in the form of snacks and convenience foods use over 1 billion pounds of chemical additives annually—about 5 pounds per person. Their purpose is to enhance the taste, and the color, to preserve, to thicken, to acidify, and to sweeten. Many of these chemicals are dangerous, untested, and absolutely unnecessary, and are suspected cause of many major and minor medical problems, such as severe allergic reactions, gastrointestinal complaints, asthma, migraines, and brain damage, as well as possibly causing carcinoma.

Nitrite

Of nitrite, one of the most dangerous additives, an article in *Medical World News,* September 7, 1973, said: "This additive, believed by critics to be the most toxic chemical in the nation's food supply, occurs in most hot dogs, bacon, ham, luncheon meats, smoked fish, and related products. Each year, more than seven billion pounds of these foods receive nitrite treatment. In cured meats, nitrite acts as a preservative, a flavoring, and a color fixative that gives them their customary bright pink color. The present-day use of sodium nitrite stems from the time-honored use of saltpeter (potassium nitrate) in cured meats. Early in the current century, scientists found that sodium nitrite was a more effective agent . . . but there have been numerous human deaths from accidental nitrite poisoning, giving this substance the dubious distinction of being the only food additive known to have caused fatalities.

"Nitrites, in the presence of stomach acid and secondary or tertiary amines, can form powerful carcinogens known as nitrosamines [cancer-causing substances]."

Monosodium Glutamate (MSG)

Millions of pounds of this chemical food additive are used to intensify the taste of food. Most of the restaurants throughout the nation add it to steaks, chops, fish, soups, and salads. So much MSG is used in Chinese restaurants that the various types of symptoms that result such as headaches, diarrhea, dermatitis, and burning sensations in the neck, forearm, and chest, are now known as the "Chinese restaurant syndrome."

The above-mentioned *Medical World News* article said this about MSG: "Subcutaneous injections of MSG damaged the central nervous system of infant mice and rats . . . along with brain damage, researchers found that some experimental animals suffered from dwarfing and obesity, learning deficits, behavioral disturbances and retinal defects."

Food Coloring

The article also commented on food colorings: "Dyes made of coal-tar derivatives are now going into the nation's foods at the rate of about 4 million pounds annually. A dozen of the dyes have been banned since 1919, when time-honored 'butter yel-

low' was found to be highly toxic and carcinogenic
. . . at present, red No. 2 (amaranth) is the most
widely used and highly suspect of the coal-tar dyes
going into food. In 1971, the FDA certified for use
more than 1.2 million pounds of the dye, which produces the vivid cherry hue of soft drinks and is also
added to ice cream, candies, baked goods and sau-
sages. A popular sugar-coated cornflake is sprayed
bright pink with red No. 2 and promoted to children
as an energy-packed breakfast."

What Can We Do about Additives?

As you can see from the above documentation, the
pervasiveness of chemical additives in practically all
of our modern foodstuffs certainly does not contribute to good nutrition, and research and actual experience have shown them to be health liabilities of both
immediate and future concern.

The medical community has started issuing warnings to the public, giving unequivocal evidence that
many diseases are caused by dietary indiscretion.
Newspapers, magazines, and medical journals are
used as media to advise the public to change their
eating habits. However, diet means restriction and de-
privation of certain foods, and psychologically that is
unacceptable to the great American public. Americans are already living in a world full of regulations
and laws, and the only remaining "pleasure" in one's
life that has no restrictions is one's eating habits. So
most Americans ignore the warnings and continue
eating as they always have.

However, the warnings of both the Food and Drug
Administration and the medical scientists have made
many in the food industry conscious of this problem.
Products are being put on the market that are free of
chemical contaminates.

All of us shiuld support these products and be criti-
cal label-readers—not only for our own immediate
safety, but to spur others in the industry to follow suit,
so that future generations will be protected from the

possible carcinogenic effects of the chemical contaminates.

Medical Schools Lack Nutrition Courses

Now that so much information is available on the
many diseases caused by nutritional transgressions,
why has the medical profession neglected to provide
proper diets for their patients, not only as a means of
treating present illnesses, but to prevent future illnesses? The answer is provided by Dr. Stanley N.
Gershoff, associate professor of nutrition at Harvard
University, who said at a recent seminar: "We found
a stream of literature on nutrition that was lousy science. We found hardly a medical school where nutrition is being seriously taught, and hardly any real-life
nutrition education going on anywhere—not to the
public, not to the professionals, not even to the doctors
or medical students." Another member of the seminar
group substantiated this statement. Dr. Dorris H.
Calloway, professor of nutrition at the University of
California at Berkeley, said: "Even here at the University of California's prestigious San Francisco Medical Center, there is no regular nutrition course for the
medical student, and the only full-time nutrition educator is on the Nursing School staff."

In the January, 1970, issue of the *Medical Tribune,*
Dr. Jean Mayer, an associate of Dr. Gershoff, stated:
"Our studies at Harvard among residents suggest that
the average physician knows a little more about nutrition than the average secretary—unless the secretary
has a weight problem. Then she probably knows more
than the average physician."

Another critic of the present-day American diet and
its morbid consequences is Dr. Alfred D. Klinger, professor of preventive medicine at Rush Medical College, who wrote in the August, 1974, issue of the
Medical Times: "Malnutrition in this country is a
malady of the first rank and is responsible in large degree for the high incidence of congenital mental
retardation, epilepsy and cerebral palsy; the high pre-
maturity rates and the seventy-five percent of all in-

fant mortality which results from it in the first month of life; the considerably higher rates of maternal morbidity; the persistent tuberculosis, bone and joint disease, heart condition, and hypertensive problems which flower from it.

"Yet there is little or no teaching of it and even less interest in nutrition, and little teaching of it in most medical and health professional schools. This is the most tragic part of the spectacle. There are those in the high circles of medicine who are agape at such a thing as malnutrition in the United States. They either deny it, or maintain that only food faddists are susceptible, or will tell you that not enough is known to do anything about it.

"As a consequence hardly any doctors know about nutrition. Few take interest in their dietary history or understand how to prescribe a proper one or correct one that is improper. Yet nutrition is the cornerstone of life. Its proper application sustains the body and the mind. Its neglect tends to cripple them."

Lack of Nutrition Training in Medical Schools Affects Physicians' Lives

The truth of Dr. Klinger's statement: "Nutrition is the cornerstone of life. Its proper application sustains the body and mind. Its neglect tends to cripple them," is manifested daily.

On one day headlines in the newspapers tell of millions dying in India of famine because of crop failures. On another day a headline states that over one million Americans are dying annually of heart and vascular diseases due to the affluent American dietary habits. These two extremes—too little and too much food—can each cause death.

Yet only one or two medical schools in the United States have recently added nutrition courses to their curricula for embryo doctors, the people who are being trained to guard our health and lives. They are launched into the practice of medicine without any knowledge of the science of nutrition. Let's see how this lack of training affects the physicians' own lives:

Dr. Emanuel Cheraskin, with a research team at the University of Alabama School of Medicine, made a study of the health of 832 physicians and their spouses over the last eight years in five American cities. He came to the conclusion that a doctor's own bad habits may influence the medical advice that he or she gives to you. The doctor who smokes is not likely to be as hard on you about the health hazards of smoking. If the doctor is fat, his or her attitude toward you if you have a weight problem will be different from that of a thin doctor. If the doctor hates to exercise, you will be less likely to learn that physical exercise can improve your health. Similarly, if the doctor does not have much knowledge of nutrition, he cannot advise you on dietary problems. As a matter of fact, most doctors do not have any specific diets that they follow. They usually eat whatever is put in front of them. As a result, they and their spouses develop the same biochemical problems. For example, in the study, male doctors with high cholesterol levels tended to have wives with similar high levels. Dr. Cheraskin said: "The similarities existed all across the board with marital similarities showing up in studies on blood sugar, enzymes, hormonal balance, and urine. I found that couples develop similar blood pressure levels after fifteen years of marriage." It was also discovered that the majority of the people in the study were overweight, and the most prevalent excuse they gave for this condition was that it was a question of genetics. "This introduced an element of hopelessness," Dr. Cheraskin states. "The fact is that in those familes everybody was eating like pigs."

How the Lack of Training in Nutrition Affected My Life

In 1931 I graduated from medical school without any training in the science of nutrition. I had given very little thought or consideration to the problem of food and its effect on the human body except that I knew that I had to eat to live and work. During the first two decades of my life I had subsisted on a more or less simple Chinese diet, consisting mainly of beef, pork, chicken, fish, vegetables, rice, and never any desserts. However, when I started to practice medicine at the age of twenty-eight, I gradually changed to a diet like that of most Americans. My usual breakfast was orange or tomato juice, ham or bacon with eggs, coffee with sugar and cream; for lunch, it would be such things as canned soup, roast beef, hot breads, sandwiches, apple pie à la mode, all washed down with a soft drink; for dinner I usually ate out at restaurants in the city. In fact, I was eating like a pig!

After seven years I had gained over forty pounds and had developed a disease known as arthritis. For three years my only relief from the agony of this disorder was the large doses of aspirin and other analgesics prescribed for me by my physicians. In addition to the wracking pains in my various joints and muscles, I developed a general dermatitis as a result of an allergy to the medication.

Several diagnoses were made of my condition, among them, rheumatoid arthritis, erosive osteoarthritis, and psoriatic arthritis. Laboratory facilities at that time were not as sophisticated as they are today, so physicians did not have the benefit of the modern tests that we have today to make a more definitive diagnosis.

My condition became progressively worse, and the last doctor I consulted, like all the others, was in a quandary. His final advice was that I should consult a psychiatrist.

I knew that I was slowly going crazy, but I wanted to think that I was not yet ready for the head-shrinker. In my desperation I remembered what my father had said to all of his nine children whenever any of us became ill: *"Bing chung how yup, woh chung how chut."* Literally translated, this means: "Sickness enters through the mouth, and catastrophe comes out of the mouth."

I had forgotten this sage folk observation in my pursuit of Western higher education and scientific knowledge. Now that all the expertise of the West had failed me, I was looking for answers elsewhere and everywhere. Perhaps I had been putting the "sickness of arthritis" into my mouth for a long time without realizing it! Thus this ancient Chinese axiom was the *revelation* that eventually rescued me from a wheelchair. It pointed me in another direction contrary to the orthodox method of treatment.

As an experiment, I went back to the Chinese "poor-man's diet" that I had been brought up on. I finally settled on seafood, vegetables, and rice as the best diet for me. To my utter amazement, in a few short weeks there was a metamorphosis. I was able to shave again, for my skin had become soft and pliable and did not weep. I was agile again, for I went from 195 to 150 pounds, which is the weight that I maintain today. I was able to play golf again, for the stiffness and pain in my joints disappeared. I was able to smile again, for the psychological torture of years was alleviated. I had almost a complete remission from my crippling disease, which has miraculously lasted until the present day.

My dramatic recovery convinced me that rheumatic diseases are caused by chemical poisoning from the chemical additives put into our food to enhance taste, smell, coloring, and for preserving; and by allergy to certain foods.

Upon returning to my medical practice, I incorporated my newly acquired knowledge of nutrition with a moderate amount of chemical therapy as a working hypothesis to treat all my patients with rheumatic diseases, and I have continued this to this day. I give them a lecture on the subject of nutrition in relation to health and illness. I warn them against the hazards of eating processed and prepared foods containing artificial flavorings, colors, chemical preservatives, and other additives. The benefits of these few minutes of conversation with my patients are immeasurable in terms of getting their cooperation and confidence. In the past thirty years or more, I have successfully treated thousands of cases of rheumatic diseases. It has been rewarding to see the high percentage of remission from pain and misery that my patients have experienced.

2

Arthritis:
Types, Causes, Treatments

It would have been usual in a book on this subject to have made this chapter on arthritis chapter 1. But as you may have gathered, I am not one to do something just because it is the usual way. Most of the other books on arthritis cover the types, causes, and treatments in detail, so if I began my book with descriptions of the various rheumatic diseases, I would not be telling you anything new. I do think such information is important to help you become better acquainted with your particular problem. But since my own treatment, which I will give details of as well as some case histories later in this chapter, is so completely tied in with diet and nutrition, I thought it important to cover that subject first.

If you are puzzled about arthritis, you are not alone. Over the years many theories and approaches have been taken in an attempt to understand this disease. My colleagues are as confused about it as you may be. Following are nine titles of recent articles on the subject which I believe will demonstrate the fact that arthritis is still an enigma.

1. "Rheumatoid Arthritis—Overlooked, Underestimated, Confusing"
2. "Joint Pain, Is it Really Rheumatoid Arthritis?"
3. "Problems in Rheumatology: Non-Articular Arthritis"

4. "Twenty-six Essentials to Differentiate Arthritis"
5. "Arthritis—Curbing the Crippler"
6. "Pain Pattern in Rheumatic Disorders"
7. "Low Back Loser Syndrome; Crippled by Pain, Hooked on Medication, Burdened by Bills"
8. "New Surgery That May Curb Arthritis"
9. "Physical Diagnosis in Rheumatoid Arthritis: It is More Certain Than X-rays and Laboratory Tests Combined"

The American Rheumatism Association lists over one hundred different arthritic conditions, but I will name and describe the symptoms of only the most common forms of rheumatic diseases. It is important that you remember that self-diagnosis is dangerous. If you recognize some symptoms, do not assume that you have one of the rheumatic diseases. Many disorders have similar symptoms—pain, inflammation, and joint involvement. For instance, these symptoms can be caused by infectious diseases such as hepatitis, tuberculosis, gonorrhea, and measles.

Rheumatoid Arthritis

Rheumatoid arthritis afflicts more than five million people in the United States, from infants to the elderly, and it is the most destructive and crippling form of arthritis. For reasons that are still unknown, it affects three times as many women as men. Rheumatoid arthritis is usually considered a systemic disease—it involves the blood vessels, the muscles, the heart, the lungs, the kidneys, and practically every other organ of the body although the joints are the prime target.

The clinical picture is characterized by joint involvement that is inflammatory, chronic, polyarthritic, and symmetrical. For instance, if the knuckles of one hand are involved, the knuckles of the other hand become involved next. Usually it does not involve the distal interphalangeal joints which means the second and third joints of the fingers are affected, but not the ends of the fingers.

In advanced cases of rheumatoid arthritis, the joints may become totally immobilized due to the severe inflammation and swelling of the synovial membranes, surrounding tissues, and muscles. The mysterious thing about rheumatoid arthritis is that often there is a remission period—that is, all the symptoms sometimes completely disappear for a period of time, only to flare up again as devastatingly as before. Most rheumatoid arthritic patients can avoid serious disability if the disease is treated in its early stages.

In children, this disorder is referred to as juvenile rheumatoid arthritis, or Still's disease after Dr. George Still, an English physician who was the first to describe it. About 6 in every 10,000 schoolchildren get some form of Still's disease, but 80 percent recover completely without ill effects. The most alarming complication of Still's disease is that it is one of the very few arthritic conditions to cause blindness. However, with proper treatment this can be prevented.

Psoriatic Arthritis and Reiter's Syndrome

These two diseases are also classified as polyarthritis of unknown etiology and have many of the characteristic features and symptoms of rheumatoid arthritis.

Osteoarthritis

Osteoarthritis, which claims approximately 10 million victims in the United States, is a degenerative disease—the wear-and-tear disease of the joints. Typically those joints that carry the most body weight are subjected to the greatest stress, and consequently the spine, the knees, and the hips are the ones affected. The wrists, the elbows, the shoulders, and the ends of the fingers can also be affected.

Although it has frequently been thought to be an old man's disease, patients have developed osteoarthritis as early as age twenty or thirty, as demonstrated by histologic evidence and X rays. However, the aching, stiffness, and creaking of the joints do not appear until middle age. Osteoarthritis is not a systemic disease, but it affects the joints locally and it goes on for years.

In severe cases the disease may destroy the normal structure of the joints. However, this is not very common, and the ends of the bones do not often grow together as in advanced cases of rheumatoid arthritis. The worst type of osteoarthritis involves the hips. Until recently this led to permanent crippling but with today's refined and improved prosthetic design and surgical techniques, total hip replacement has given comfort and mobility to many otherwise hopeless cases.

Ankylosing Spondylitis

Ankylosing spondylitis is one of the more common rheumatic diseases and there are approximately 1 million cases in the United States. It occurs in men ten times as often as in women, and it usually begins in the early twenties and middle age. This is a chronic inflammatory disease. The inflammation most often starts at the sacroiliac joints and gradually spreads up the spine toward the neck. Occasionally, other joints—the shoulders, the hips, and the knees —are affected. It differs from rheumatoid arthritis in that the inflammation is normally confined to the spine, and seldom to the joints of the limbs. In severe cases of ankylosing spondylitis the eyes, heart, and intestines are occasionally involved. In diagnosing this disease, X rays of the spine are essential for they reveal the disorder in its very early states as well as in its later progression.

Gout

Most of us are familiar with gout. We know more about this disease than all the other types of arthritis—yet there are over 1 million people in the United

States suffering from it today. It is called the "snob" form of arthritis, because it is common among the wealthy and successful segments of the population.

In fact, a caricature of the gourmand, King Henry VIII, often seen in comic strips, is a picture description of gout that is worth 10,000 words. King Henry is shown as a fat, well-groomed monarch sitting on a great chair with his leg, bandaged and with a big, red, inflamed toe exposed, resting on a footstool. In one hand he holds a large rib of beef and in the other hand a mug of ale.

At a recent seminar in New Zealand, I learned that when the native Maoris deserted their traditional fish-and-vegetable diet for the "white man's" one of beef, lamb, candies, and dairy products, they developed obesity, cardiovascular diseases, and numerous cases of gout.

This confirms the long-known fact that gout is a metabolic disease and that dietary transgression is one of its main causes. People with gout and gouty arthritis usually have high uric acid content in their blood. The foods that contain the most uric acid are brains, sweetbreads, kidneys, liver, meat extracts, sardines, anchovies, and caviar. Since the consumption of too many alcoholic beverages injures the kidneys and prevents the body from getting rid of the uric acid, people who eat and drink excessively are prone to have gout.

The symptoms of gout, inflammation and swelling of the involved joints, make it the most painful of all arthritic diseases. The big toe is usually the target area, but other parts of the body may also become involved. In severe cases of gout, the kidneys can be damaged by uric acid. Kidney stones sometimes form, causing agonizing pains and threatening life itself, for the kidney is then unable to eliminate waste products.

Modern research has given us a great deal of knowledge concerning the treatment of gout. The orthodox method today is the use of the following medication: (1) Indocin, Butazolidin, and Tandearil, successful drugs for relieving the acute pain of gout;

(2) probenecid, a drug used to increase the elimination of uric acid; (3) allopurinol, a new and effective drug used to reduce the formation of uric acid in the body, which should be taken indefinitely.

The success of these drugs in the treatment of gout has resulted in a tendency among physicians to forget to emphasize dietary measures. In my treatment of gout, dietary restrictions are of the utmost importance. Many of my patients are allergic to the medications used to control gout. If those patients whom I have put on a diet stray from it, they come back to my office and say, "It is too painful to cheat. I've learned my lesson!"

I consider it unnecessary for patients to have to rely on drugs alone for the rest of their lives, when the same results can be accomplished by mere discipline.

Connective-Tissue Disorders

Connective tissue essentially binds together and is the support of the various structures of the body. There are three types made up of protein fibrils—collagen, reticulin, and elastin. Connective-tissue disorders are thought to be due to autoimmunity—a form of allergy. Autoimmunity, as I discuss further in Chapter 4, means that something goes wrong with the antibodies we have in our bodies to protect us from infections, and instead of fighting invading bacteria and viruses, they somehow attack the body's own tissue.

Inflammation, swelling, and pain caused by autoimmunity may occur in all parts of the body, including the lungs, the skin, the heart, and the kidneys, as well as the joints.

The diseases included in this category are:

1. *Systemic lupus erythematosus.* This condition has all the above symptoms and is often mistaken for rheumatoid arthritis although new laboratory techniques have been able to defin-

itively separate these two diseases. Systemic lupus erythematosus attacks more women than men.

2. *Polyarteritis nodosa.* This is an inflammation of the small and medium-size blood vessels throughout the body.

3. *Scleroderma.* In this disease the skin of the patient throughout the body thickens considerably and becomes hard and rigid with pigmented patches. Scleroderma can also involve the heart, the kidneys, and the lungs.

4. *Dermatomyositis.* This is also a systemic disease involving the skin, muscles, and connective tissue. The skin usually shows swelling and thickening, and the muscles become swollen, tender, and weak. Approximately 70 percent of the victims of this disease are female, and it usually occurs after forty years of age.

Nonarticular Arthritis

Of the 50 million people with rheumatic diseases, 20 million are victims of the articular type of diseases previously mentioned—rheumatoid arthritis, osteoarthritis, ankylosing spondylitis, and also collagen diseases (which affect mainly the joints). The other 30 million fall into the nonarticular category, which is often called soft-tissue rheumatism. Joint inflammation is not usually present.

The American Rheumatism Association classifies the following conditions as nonarticular rheumatism: fibrositis, intervertebral disc and low-back syndromes, myositis and myalgia, tendinitis and peritendinitis (bursitis), tenosynovitis, fasciitis, carpal tunnel syndrome, and others.

From this classified nomenclature you can see that the principal areas of affliction are the muscles, the tendons, the bursae, the joint capsules, and other types of fibrous tissues, fat, and nerves. In other words, all the tissues from the head down to the feet are involved. These are the commonest and mildest forms of rheumatic diseases. Also included are such common conditions as bursitis, stiff neck, backaches, and muscle spasms. Very few people go through life without having been attacked by one form or another of this group of rheumatic diseases, and most people do not usually consult doctors. They rely on home remedies, which normally take care of the majority of these disorders.

Modern Theories as to the Cause of Arthritis

One can gather from the above discussion that arthritis is not a single disease but a group of over one hundred disease entities and syndromes. These ailments date back to antiquity—Pleistocene man, who lived 500,000 years ago, was found to have had osteoarthritis in his skeletal remains. The well-preserved Egyptian mummies showed that many of those people had rheumatic diseases. Medical books of ancient China mentioned and described arthritis and the use of acupuncture as a mode of treatment. It is natural, then, that physicians throughout the centuries have propounded many theories as to the cause of rheumatic diseases—and have invented multitudes of methods and medicines for their cure.

For some reason, the medical profession in the United States has been apathetic toward this group of diseases. Only during the past twenty-five years has special attention been given to the study of arthritis, yet it is the nation's third-ranking cause of disability. Intensive efforts and millions of dollars are now being expended to discover the cause, prevention, and possible cure of the rheumatic diseases. The greatest efforts are being channeled into the study of rheumatoid arthritis, because it is the second-largest category of the rheumatic group. In the United States there are over 5 million victims. To emphasize the pervasiveness of this disease, think of San Francisco, which has a population of 700,000, and six other cities of the same size, completely populated by victims of rheumatic diseases.

Since rheumatoid arthritis is the most crippling form of the inflammatory illnesses, medical scientists feel that if its etiology or origins can be discovered, other rheumatic diseases will subsequently be conquered.

Of the many modern theories as to the cause of rheumatoid arthritis, the following are the most prominent ones:

1. Rheumatoid arthritis is caused by bacteria or viruses.
2. Rheumatoid arthritis is due to the abnormality of the body's defense system—the autoimmune theory.
3. Rheumatoid arthritis is caused by a combination of the two items above.
4. Rheumatoid arthritis is due to psychiatric or emotional factors.
5. Rheumatoid arthritis is caused by metabolic and biochemical factors.

1. Rheumatoid Arthritis Is Caused by Bacteria or Viruses

The oldest of the modern theories is the infection theory. At one time it was thought that the same organism that caused tuberculosis was also responsible for rheumatoid arthritis. Thus, gold salt injections, used at that time for the treatment of TB, were also used for the treatment of rheumatoid arthritis. There are diseases that sometimes, in a low percentage of the cases, can cause arthritis as part of their symptom-complex. Arthritis can be caused by streptococci, gonococci, pneumococci, the syphilis spirochete, tubercle bacilli, and other bacteria and therefore, this seems to support the infection theory. When the disease is cured, the arthritic symptoms disappear because the toxins (poisons) from the disease are eliminated. Recently, a member of my family developed pain and swelling in her joints resembling an acute case of rheumatoid arthritis. She was hospitalized and on thorough examination was found to have hepatitis.

In curing her hepatitis, her arthritis symptoms disappeared. This is the reason why people with joint pains should see their own physician to determine whether it is caused by an infectious type of arthritis, or is due to rheumatoid arthritis and other types listed in this chapter, for which no cause has been found to date.

I remember that in 1929, when I was taking my clinical training in medical school, my professor of orthopedics was one of those zealous scientists who believed that arthritis was caused by a focus of infection. He thought that the infection could be located somewhere else, such as in the gallbladder, the appendix, the tonsils, or the teeth. The infectious organism would then somehow enter the bloodstream, localizing in the various joints, causing inflammation, and resulting in arthritis. It was believed that arthritis could be cured, then, by removing the focus of the infection.

For several years many normal gallbladders, tonsils, and appendixes were removed and healthy sets of teeth were extracted in the hope of curing arthritis.

In fact, when I had arthritis, one of my many consultants suggested the removal of all my teeth. Fortunately, I did not heed his advice, and I still have my own teeth today.

Many researchers are looking for a virus, which they think is the cause of arthritis. Many viruses and viruslike particles have been found in the joints of arthritic victims, but none of these viruses has been shown to be the cause of the disease. No microorganism has been isolated as the causative factor of rheumatoid arthritis.

2. Rheumatoid Arthritis Is Due to the Abnormality of the Body's Defense System —Autoimmune Theory

This theory postulates that the body's defense system, for unaccountable reasons, reacts against its own tissues in the joints, causing the lining of the joints to become inflamed and damaged. This is called an autoimmune reaction.

This theory as to the cause of arthritis has been accepted as the "working hypothesis" for research during the past three decades. Most medical scientists believe that the inciting organism initiating the whole process is a virus that they have not yet found. However, Dr. Charles M. Plotz, a famous rheumatologist, stated in the *Medical World News* of April, 1974: "The concept of autoimmunity in rheumatoid arthritis is open to criticism . . . my guess is that the disease really isn't autoimmune, but that some extrinsic factor is involved." Dr. Plotz's concept agrees with my theory. My extrinsic factors are food allergens and chemical additives. (See allergy, chapter 4 for further discussion of this theory.)

3. Rheumatoid Arthritis Is Caused by a Combination of the Above Items 1 and 2

Item 1: This theory suggests the following etiology —that some bacteria invaded the joints, causing damage to the tissue, changing its character, thus making the defense system "think" that the tissue is not its own but a foreign body.

Item 2: The defense system then develops antibodies against the joint tissues.

4. Psychiatric or Emotional Factors as the Cause of Rheumatoid Arthritis

One of the most interesting observations in this theory is made by Dr. A. Johnson, whose studies suggest that more arthritics may have psychiatric disorders than was previously believed. The following is a quote from *The Geigy Clinical Forum on Arthritis* (this particular case was cited by Dr. Johnson to exemplify those cases of rheumatoid arthritis which bear the closest resemblance to what is known as conversion hysteria): "One of the more bizarre cases in the annals of rheumatoid arthritis is that of the woman who had been accused by her husband of infidelity and rapidly developed arthritis in the ring finger. This disease soon spread to all the fingers of both hands.

"Whatever our ultimate knowledge may be about the origins and course of this disease, psychiatric disorders have been diagnosed in a large proportion of the arthritic patients who have been studied comprehensively during the past two decades. Information about this body of data, and associated hypotheses, may be helpful to physicians, particularly in understanding and managing arthritic patients in whom psychological problems are suggested."

By and large, rheumatologists reject the idea that the psychiatric factor is the main cause of rheumatoid arthritis. Although all physicians who treat chronic diseases recognize that there is always a psychological involvement in every case, the question is whether it is the cause or the result of the disease. It is difficult to differentiate between them.

5. Metabolic and Biochemical Factors as the Cause of Rheumatoid Arthritis

The only theory that has not been investigated to any extent is the one that says metabolic and biochemical factors (food allergens and chemical additives) are the cause of rheumatoid arthritis.

The reason for this is that the Arthritis Foundation, which is the leading authority on the subject of rheumatic diseases, has flatly stated: "The relationship between diet and arthritis has been thoroughly and scientifically studied. The simple proven fact is: no food has anything to do with causing arthritis and no food is effective in treating or 'curing' it."

Yet the next line of the foundation's booklet, *Arthritis—the Basic Facts,* reads: "The one exception is with gouty arthritis. Certain foods increase uric acid levels in the body and should be avoided."

Isn't this contradictory? If one kind of arthritis is

caused by food, then why not other kinds of arthritis?

If I had not been afflicted with this disease and faced with the possibility of being crippled for the rest of my life, I might have accepted their authoritative statements, and certainly I would not be writing this book.

The Arthritis Foundation has a responsibility to the public and to the members of the medical profession who rely upon its pronouncements. It seems to me that its members may have accepted, without proof, the hypothesis that diet has no relationship to arthritis. Their statement that this relationship has been thoroughly and scientifically studied cannot be true. My clinical observations contradict this. It is to the detriment of the foundation and the general public to prevent further research along this line.

How Physicians Diagnose Rheumatoid Arthritis

Psychological factors play a very important part in our lives. When medical students are introduced to the study of a new disease in clinical practice, they frequently relate the disease to their personal lives. I recall a fellow student who had kidney trouble when we studied the kidney diseases, lung trouble when we studied the lung diseases, and stomach trouble when we studied the gastrointestinal problems.

If you should have some aches and pains after reading the chapter on rheumatic diseases, don't diagnose yourself as having arthritis, but perhaps you should go to have that long-neglected physical examination.

But if you have pains, stiffness, and inflammation of the joints over a period of several weeks, don't just take aspirin or other medication to relieve the pains (as we all see on the TV commercials)—this may indicate the first symptoms of rheumatoid arthritis. Do go to see your personal physician.

When a rheumatoid arthritic patient consults a physician, his first complaints will be of pain, stiffness, and swelling of several weeks' duration.

What joints are involved, whether the involvement

is symmetrical, unusual fatigue, loss of strength, and morning stiffness that lasts for at least a thirty-minute period are all clues in the history of the patient that indicate rheumatoid arthritis.

Laboratory Examinations

After a thorough physical examination, the patient is sent for a series of laboratory examinations to confirm the clinical findings of the doctor. Normally the erythrocyte sedimentation rate (ESR) is elevated, and this is an index of the severity of the arthritis. The latex fixation test is useful in determining the rheumatoid factor in the serum of the patient's blood. The most important of all the laboratory tests is the one that aspirates (draws out) the fluid from the joints for examination. This gives much information to substantiate the rheumatic disease.

Other laboratory tests, such as antinuclear antibody test (ANA), total complement test, and immunoelecrophoresis (IEP) test, help the physician in his differential diagnosis—to distinguish rheumatoid arthritis from other types of arthritis.

In the early stages of rheumatoid arthritis, X-ray examination does not reveal much, but in severe cases of six months' duration, erosion of the joints will appear in the film.

The history, physical examination, and laboratory test results will usually give the physician a comprehensive picture of the arthritic condition of the patient. The doctor can then proceed with his treatment program.

Therapy and Management of Arthritis

A government survey in 1970 showed that the annual direct cost of medical care for arthritic patients was as follows:

| | Cost (in millions |
| | of dollars) |
Care	
Hospitalization	$854
Physicians' office visits	493
"Quackery" products	408
Prescription drugs	600
Nonprescription drugs	500
Other than physician services	50
Federal and private programs for arthritis	26
Total:	$2,931

In 1966 the same direct cost of medical care was one-third as much. These statistics also showed that in that year there were 17 million arthritic victims in the United States, and in less than five years, in 1970, the total had increased to 20,230,000 victims—so, obviously, whatever method of treatment the medical world is using to prevent and cure rheumatic diseases is ineffective.

The following treatment program is the one that is followed by most physicians in the treatment of rheumatoid arthritis:

1. In the beginning stages of the disease, the emphasis is on the relief of pain, prevention of inflammation and deformities, and maintenance of function. The family and the rheumatoid arthritis patient are warned they must have a long-term outlook toward the treatment. Aspirin is considered the best treatment because it stops the pain and reduces inflammation. Very large doses are given to the patient—as many as 12 to 25 tablets a day.

2. If the patient does not respond to the treatment, and the disease continues, becoming moderately severe, affecting multiple joints, and causing considerable physical disturbance and disability, then further measures are added to the basic regimen. Other types of medication given are: phenylbutazone, indomethacin, antimalarials,

and intra-articular steroids. At the same time, intensive physical and occupational therapy and orthopedic devices, such as splints, bars, and canes, are used.

3. If the rheumatoid arthritis patient should fail to respond adequately to these measures, then oral steroids and gold treatments are given. There are many side effects to these chemical agents, and some doctors prefer not to use them. Gold is a potent antiarthritic agent and has been in clinical use for almost fifty years, but its toxicity and side effects are formidable. A blood count, platelet count, and urinalysis should be taken frequently while the rheumatoid arthritis patient is undergoing gold therapy.

4. About 35 percent of the rheumatoid arthritis patients get well with almost no recurrences, about 50 percent continue to be afflicted with occasional remissions and recurrences, and 15 percent are severe cases and have no remissions at all. Hands, feet, and hips become deformed and crippled, and surgical measures are resorted to for the patient's comfort and function.

5. Those patients who are unresponsive to the conventional therapy are then given experimental medication—immunosuppressive drugs or cytotoxic agents such as cyclophosphamide, chlorambucil, azathioprine, D-penicillamine, histidine, dimethyl-sulfoxide, radioactive gold, and aryl acids (mefenamic, fluenamic).

Drug-Oriented America

Although the number of victims of rheumatoid arthritis has gradually increased during the past two decades, the conventional method of treatment has not changed much, except that many new medications have been introduced to treat the symptoms. The present generation of physicians seem drug-oriented, their one goal being to find more and better drugs as the panacea for the rheumatic diseases.

Recently a new drug, ibuprofen, was introduced. In a yearlong experiment involving about 1,000 patients, ibuprofen showed effectiveness comparable to that of aspirin, but with fewer gastrointestinal problems. This drug is not a cure—it only suppresses the symptoms like aspirin. A recent check on the cost of ibuprofen in the San Francisco area revealed that the price is $17 per 100 tablets, while 250 tablets of aspirin cost only $1. And the druggist mentioned that the pharmaceutical house is already six weeks behind in orders for it.

If there is any need to substantiate the fact that physicians are drug-oriented, the backlog of orders for this new drug shows it clearly. Other companies are hurrying to put out similar drugs.

Aspirin

In the United States about 15,000 tons of aspirin are produced and consumed annually. Although aspirin is considered a safe drug, the large doses that are prescribed for rheumatoid arthritis patients often create serious consequences.

Dr. Harvey J. Weiss, professor of medicine at Columbia University, stated in the *Journal of the American Medical Association* of August 26, 1974: "Ingestion of aspirin, in doses of 1 to 3 gm/day, will induce occult gastrointestinal bleeding in about 70% of normal subjects. This generally amounts to a daily fecal blood loss of approximately 5 ml (normal loss is less than 1 ml), although much greater losses have been recorded in some individuals. In habitual aspirin users, occult gastrointestinal bleeding may result in an iron-deficiency anemia. More serious are the reports that aspirin ingestion can cause acute and massive gastric hermorrhage.

"Aspirin-induced asthma is by far the most serious of the adverse reactions . . . [A small percentage of aspirin takers develop a hypersensitivity, and according to Dr. Weiss.] . . . death may occur within minutes after ingestion of the drug unless appropriate measures are instituted immediately.

"Aspirin has also been implicated in causing various types of skin eruptions, transient albuminuria, nephrotoxicity and thrombocytopenia. In addition, aspirin ranks second only to barbiturates among drugs used for the purpose of suicide. Aspirin overdose is still a frequent cause of accidental poisoning in children."

Since my illness some thirty years ago, when I was given 4 to 5 grams of aspirin a day (equivalent to 12 or 15 tablets), I have been reluctant to prescribe any large dose of aspirin to my patients and I immediately cut down to the lowest possible dose what they have been taking. In my opinion, every doctor who empirically prescribes such large doses to his patients, because some authority said to do it, should first be made to experiment on himself with 15 aspirins a day for a week or longer to see what reactions he gets to this supposedly "safe" drug. After the week's trial with the aspirin, I am sure he would be hesitant about prescribing such large doses to *any* patient over a period of months or years.

In the next few pages, I present some case histories of patients with the various rheumatic diseases who were treated with my dietary regimen, with moderate doses of medication and with acupuncture. These cases are typical of those I treat, and I want to emphasize the fact that every one of my patients is a chronic case for all patients who come to my office are screened. If their arthritis is of recent origin, I advise them to go to their local physicians or rheumatologist for examination and treatment. If they have been suffering for years, then I consider them as potential patients, because they present a challenge to me. Each has had extensive laboratory tests of every kind and X rays to substantiate that they are afflicted with one of the rheumatic disorders. They bring in histories taken over a period of several years, so that it is not necessary for me to subject them to further tests unless those they've had are not of recent date. Each patient also brings in with him or her vials of colored pills and vitamins and aspirin in every form.

I have presented these case histories in an informal manner so the patients can express their own emotions about the problems of their disease. As you read about their personal experiences, you will then understand the problems that typical victims of arthritis face every day of their lives.

INTERVIEW TAPED ON MARCH 1, 1974

[Mrs. V. W. is a fifty-seven-year-old housewife who came into my office in March, 1973, for the treatment of rheumatoid arthritis. This tape was made on March 1, 1974, one year from the time she started her treatments with me.]

"Two years ago, while I was playing golf, a golfer on the next fairway sliced a ball and struck me in the chest with it. I was taken to the hospital where they found that I had two fractured ribs. They even thought I had a heart attack. But about a week later, it turned out that I had arthritis in my ribs and not a heart attack, because my left knee started to get swollen and very painful too. Then the pain went up to my hips. My sister, who is an internist at the University of California Hospital sent me to be taken care of by a rheumatologist. He gave me the whole works, all the examinations, blood work, EKG and all kinds of other tests. He diagnosed my condition as rheumatoid arthritis. He gave me a shot of cortisone in my chest because that was where I had the severe pains. He also gave me injections in my knees. But the knee got so swollen that they had to drain it twice. My condition became worse, I could not walk up the stairs at all. If the elevator was out in our apartment building, I had to stay indoors all day. I could not get in and out of bed by myself. I could not take a bath by myself. It was difficult for me to get in and out of a chair. Riding in an automobile was most painful—I hurt all over. The doctor gave me heavy doses of aspirins, cortisone, and Indocin, which helped me some.

"About that time my husband retired, so we decided to move to Coronado, where the weather was better and warmer. My sister recommended another rheumatologist down there to take care of me. I had to go through all the examinations again. This doctor put me on the same medication. My general condition became worse. I had so much pain I could hardly do anything. In addition, I was taking so much cortisone that I acquired an ugly moon face.

[The patient was put on the Dong Diet. I explained to her my theory that her rheumatoid arthritis was probably due to food allergy and allergy to the chemical additives in her food. She was admonished to adhere strictly to the diet.

Since the patient had been taking large doses of medication for quite a while, it was necessary to gradually decrease the medication as she improved. After two days of dieting, the patient was given four consecutive daily acupuncture treatments in my office.

She responded very well to this therapy program. Her pains decreased and she lost approximately seven pounds. On March 29, 1973, Mrs. W. was instructed to return to her home in Coronado to rest. She was instructed to keep in touch with me by telephone. One week later, she telephoned to tell me that she felt much better and that she had lost more weight. At this point, I instructed her to decrease the dosage of her medication by one-half. Two weeks later, she phoned me to report that her pains had completely disappeared.

On May 17, 1973, Mrs. W. returned to my office for further treatment. She walked into my office without help. She was pain-free. She weighed 139 pounds, having lost 27 pounds since I first began treating her, on March 23, 1973.

Due to some residual swelling and stiffness in her joints, I continued to give the patient acupuncture treatment on that basis once a month, until March 1, 1974, when the patient was discharged.]

"Today I am 126 pounds. During the last five months I have taken about five cortisone tablets only. I used to take five every day, together with about 20 aspirins a day. Now I do not take any aspirins at all. I ride around Coronado on a bicycle and my friends think that I am crazy to go to see a doctor any more. My husband is very proud of me now and said it was just like a new honeymoon."

INTERVIEW TAPED ON AUGUST 23, 1974

[Mrs. C. B., age thirty-nine, a housewife, came into my office for treatments in June, 1973, complaining of being severely ill with rheumatoid arthritis since the age of twenty-one. At that time she started having symptoms of aches and pains in her knees and ankles from time to time. She went to several doctors, who only gave her pills to take without any definite diagnosis. These intermittent pains and aches lasted for about ten years, until one night in 1961, Carol woke up in the middle of the night with a sudden exacerbation of her symptoms.]

"It was in 1961 when I went to bed one night, perfectly normal with no indication of anything wrong, then, in the middle of the night I was awakened with my hands completely distorted and my arms as stiff as boards and they felt like something was going up and down in them. I was screaming because I had such excruciating pains. Our family doctor was called, and he diagnosed it as muscle spasms. He gave me some pills and told me to stay in bed and rest. I did not get any better, so he finally sent me to a hospital to find out what was exactly wrong with me. After several days they told me that I had rheumatoid arthritis.

"Then they started treatments on me. They gave me medicines and followed up with physio-therapy. I was in and out of the Presbyterian Hospital where they gave me the hot-wax treatment on my hands and feet; then at other times they gave me ice packs; you just name it, they tried everything. For starters they gave me thirty aspirins a day, which needless to say, ruined my stomach. I had repercussions from that and got very sick. So they stopped that treatment and then had me on Darvon. They gave me gold shots also. They must have tried just about every medication that there is associated with this disease. I was sort of a guinea pig for pills. Then they gave me cortisone shots, which also did not work. Finally, they gave me prednisone and Percodan, and also aspirin again, which seemed to be the best combination for me. I had to take these pills all the time in order to stop the stiffness, and the pains and aches.

"In 1962 even though I was still suffering from the disease I married a wonderful man who had stood by me all these years. I could hardly walk down the aisle of the church for that day was the first time in a year that I wore shoes.

"I was determined to have a baby to make some-thing meaningful of my life and to have someone to share life with. The rheumatologist told us that during pregnancy I might not have any symptoms of the rheumatoid arthritis, but I was not one of the lucky ones. I had to continue on with the medication in or-der to have my baby.

"So we had Lisa, a cesarean baby. It was tough, but we made it. During the six-week checkup, the doctor found that I had cancer of the cervix, so I had to have a hysterectomy. From then on my arthritis became worse even though I was taking the various medicines. My hands, knees, and feet became deformed and I had to have a series of operations.

"My first operation was on my hands, then my knees. In fact, I had both my hands and my knees operated on within six months' time because it was so bad. Then my toes separated from my metatarsal bone and they had to reconstruct one foot, and at the same time they did a double bunionectomy. Then they repaired the tendons of the right foot, hoping that the toes would not separate. After that they asked me to have another operation. This was the straw that broke the camel's back! After going through all those opera-tions they said that I should have my left elbow oper-ated on because of the terrible pains I had in it. They said that it was due to calcium deposits. The only thing that they could do was to go in and scrape the elbow, like they did to my hands. No guarantee that it would be well. I told my husband that I would not have any more surgery.

"Just about that time I heard about Dr. Dong and his treatment with arthritis.

[Mrs. B. was put on the Dong Diet. She was told that she should strictly adhere to the diet plan. She had been taking the following medication, prescribed by her former physician: 30 aspirins a day, prednisone (15 mgs.), Butazolidin, and Percodan when the pain became too severe. One week later, the patient returned to my office. Prior to her first acupuncture treatment, it was necessary for her to have assistance in undressing. The nurse and her husband assisted her and the three of us lifted her on to the examination table.

She continued to follow her diet rigidly. She was given acupuncture therapy once or twice a month, according to her degree of improvement. Also, her medication was gradually decreased as she began to feel better. The patient lost 32 pounds. She was free of pain.]

"It used to be that I could not even use the vacuum cleaner without having repercussions for about two days. I have a great deal of stamina now. In fact, in the fall of 1973, my husband and I painted the whole house, inside and outside.

"I do not take any aspirin now and I only take 3 mg. prednisone a day, and I am now trying to cut that down. But I am adhering strictly to the diet. I got off a few times and got sick. Never again!"

INTERVIEW TAPED ON MARCH 8, 1974

[Mrs. A. W. is a thirty-nine-year-old school-teacher.]

"I have had rheumatoid arthritis for about ten years, since 1963. While working at the local school, I hit my wrist on a towel bin and I thought that I had broken it. I had x-rays taken and they showed that nothing was broken. The pains went from my wrist down to my knuckles and fingers and soon my left hand was bothering me and I could not tolerate the pain at all.

"I decided to come down to San Francisco to go to a good internist that we had heard about. This doctor diagnosed it as rheumatoid arthritis, after extensive examinations. He told me to take aspirin tablets until I heard bells ring and then to cut back on the amount of aspirin that I took. That was about all that he said could be done for it. So I continued on with this treatment, but with constant pains in various joints and stiffness in my arms and legs, especially in the mornings.

"I became pregnant with my first child. While I was pregnant the problem with the pain went away. My second pregnancy in 1965 was the same way; during the time I was pregnant, I had almost no trouble. But after the baby was born, the pain came right back and it got progressively worse. At times my joints would be so inflamed that I would have to crawl around the house. I could not put any weight on them at all; but I had responsibilities with my family and I had to do the work the best way that I knew how, so I continued to take large doses of aspirins in order to be able to do this work.

"In 1969, when the pains became so bad that I could not stand it any longer, I was recommended to see another specialist in San Francisco, a famous rheumatologist. He confirmed that I had rheumatoid arthritis after examining me and repeating many laboratory tests. He decided that I was taking too many aspirins and that there was something better for me. I tried his new medicine for a while, but it did not agree with me. So I went back to the aspirin for pain.

"A new teacher came to school who had arthritis. He had been treated by a doctor in Mexico. Since I was going on vacation with my family in Baja and would be passing through this town in Mexico, I decided to try this method of treatment.

"I consulted with this doctor in Mexico and he gave me medication that I kept on for three years. All the joints went down in size. But after a while, I had some bad reactions. The skin from my knees down to the ankles became very thin and if I would knock my knees on a table or any object that was solid, it would break open like a watermelon. I became very alarmed.

"I went to the University of California Hospital in San Francisco for a week's stay. They told me that it was the massive doses of steroids that I had been taking from the doctor in Mexico. They made me go off these steroids immediately. As I was going off the medication my knees ballooned up and my joints just flared up and I even got nodules on my elbows, hard nodules. I was very sick. I could not bend my knees because they were so inflamed. I could not walk up or down the stairs because of the pains. My husband had to get me out of bed in the morning, and also out of anything that was low, like a chair or the car. I could not sit in a chair that did not have arms so I could push or pull myself out of it.

"I consider myself a very capable person, I can do anything that I make up my mind to do, but this rheumatoid arthritis was getting to a point where I was not able to manage for myself. I know that I would have been in a wheelchair if I did not have two children to take care of. I am not the kind of person to give up, but I was very close to the point of giving up after I left the University of California Hospital.

[During Mrs. W.'s first visit, she was put on the Dong Diet and warned to adhere to it rigidly. She weighed 170 pounds and was grossly overweight for her age and height. She was told to restrict her intake of carbohydrates.

Her medication had consisted of 24 aspirin tablets a day, prescribed by her previous physician. These did not curb either the pain or the inflammation of her joints. She was almost completely helpless. Subse-

quently the patient was given one acupuncture treatment a month for six months.

The patient responded to the therapy program amazingly well. She lost forty pounds and was completely pain-free.]

"As long as I stay on the diet I feel great. The minute that I deviate either by mistake, or otherwise, I find that I have pain and I know it immediately. Now I am back to my teaching job, and I am happy again. I am not taking any medication at all except an aspirin once in a while, when I occasionally get a pain.

"Last week the children of my class and I had a race to the classroom door. That is something that I had not been able to do for ten years."

Review and Comment

In thinking about these three cases, I am reminded of Shakespeare's sage but unscientific remark: "Desperate diseases require desperate measures." The attending physicians on these cases seem to have been carrying this out. The prognosis of all three was practically hopeless. Each woman had been treated by specialists and superspecialists, in clinics and superclinics. Moreover, there were further disadvantages. These patients had been warned by the Arthritis Foundation handbook: "It is extremely important to understand that the major forms of arthritis are chronic. This means the condition, once started, continues usually for life. It means that one does not 'heal up as good as new,' as after the common cold, measles or a cut in the skin. It means that whatever damage takes place remains permanently . . . and tends to get worse unless proper precautions are taken to prevent it. It means treatment must continue on and on."

Was it idiotic of me to try to salvage these hopeless cases when so many specialists had failed? Should I have sent them home with large doses of aspirin to wait for some medical scientist to make the "break-through" that has been promised year after year since 1948, or to wait for the spontaneous remissions that rheumatologists have frequently talked about?

It is now history that these three "hopeless" cases have recovered from the depths of their mental and physical despair. The victory was attained by the full overall performance and cooperation not only of the patients but also of their families in following the therapeutic program that I outlined for them.

Now Mrs. A. W. is teaching school again and racing the children to the door. Mrs. C. B. has painted her house, and Mrs. V. W. is riding her bicycle all around Coronado, waving to her friends, who think she is slightly crazy to fly up to San Francisco to see her doctor anymore. They may not "heal up as good as new," but they are certainly pretty good imitations of new personalities.

Why didn't these women get well with all the "supertreatment" that they had received? Why didn't they get that "spontaneous remission" during all those treatments in the past? I think that the fault lies in the fragmentation of our medical system. Scientific and technological advances in medicine have increased knowledge so extensively that it necessitates the formation of groups of specialists and superspecialists in every field. The drawback of this is that the human body is divided into many parts for the study and treatment of rheumatic diseases, with the result that doctors forget that there is a total human being. A comic once said that when his nose cold went down into his chest, he had to change doctors to cure it. There is a great deal of truth in that statement.

Among the other shortcomings of the treatments that prevented the women's recovery were these three outstanding factors: (1) the patients were not given a sensible dietary program—they were allowed to put any type of food and drink into bodies that were already enfeebled by their chronic disease; (2) the patients were allowed to acquire another disease—obesity—for each one of them gained thirty to forty pounds. This excess weight not only encumbered their already diseased joints but also promoted eventual hypertension, vascular and heart disease, diabetes, and other nutrition-related diseases; (3) large doses of aspirin and other toxic drugs were prescribed over long periods of time. Aspirin, as described by Dr. Weiss, even though useful, has many drawbacks. It has caused gastrointestinal diseases such as ulcers, gastritis, internal bleeding, kidney malfunction, colon ulceration, loss of taste, and eye trouble.

Overviewing the entire medical spectrum, the discipline of rheumatology, full of ambiguities and polemics, is the one discipline that needs a little creative heresy and dissent—for 20 million seriously ill arthritic victims are waiting for a few answers to their agonies instead of 20 aspirin every day.

The Arthritis Foundation has spent many millions of dollars and many years of research on the rheumatic diseases. Why haven't they reached their goal of "both prevention and cure"? Possibly because of a long-standing obsession. The elite members, as brilliant young medical students, were bacteriologically oriented, and seemingly they cannot break away from that inculcation. Their whole research program is geared toward finding some viruses or infectious organisms as the cause of arthritis, or of finding that rheumatic diseases are caused by some overaction of the body's immunity in the defense system, possibly initiated by infection with a virus or a mycobacteria. Probably their research funding for "young scientists" is earmarked for projects that fit in with their master plan of searching for viruses or bacteria. I suspect that if a young scientist dared to ask for a grant to pursue his own ideas, such as whether or not there is a correlation between nutrition and arthritis, he would be thrown out of the foundation's offices.

I think it was Confucius who said, "To oppose authoritarianism is not only a strategic necessity but a spiritual imperative." This is a beautiful philosophy, but to oppose authority is to live in a lonely world—as I have with my dietary hypothesis—and suffer the indignities of all iconoclasts. But for me, to be able to give a new outlook in life to these three women and others like them is sufficient inspiration to continue on with my work. The prolonged suffering of these victims had extended adversely into the lives and life-style of their families and friends. Their recovery has lifted a heavy responsibility and burden from their loved ones, which makes me doubly happy.

These incidents, together with thousands of inspiring letters from all over the country, and now from many of my medical colleagues, have given my spirits a new lift.

3

How the Chemicals in Our Food Poison Our Bodies

Let's return for a minute to Fantasyland. Keep in mind the fact that we are made up of 60 trillion bricks and that each one of these bricks is alive and functioning. When John Jones became intoxicated, he overloaded himself with alcohol that his liver could not detoxify. This resulted in the poisoning of trillions of his bricks, which made him drunk, inebriated, intoxicated, or whatever term one chooses to describe the mental and physical condition he was in. Perhaps the best word to describe his condition is sick!

Following this logic, my theory and my contention is that the thousands of chemical substances that are routinely added to our foods and ingested by us cause poisoning and damage to the trillions of joint bricks and other tissue bricks surrounding the joints, resulting in a disturbance of function, which we call arthritis. For poison as defined in *Dorland's Medical Dictionary* is "any substance which, when ingested, inhaled or absorbed, or when applied to, injected into, or developed within the body, in relatively small accounts, by its chemical action *may cause damage to structure or disturbance of function.*" (Italics mine.)

In the case of John Jones, the alcohol had an affinity for his brain bricks, causing his loss of equilibrium. In the case of victims of arthritis, various toxic substances have an affinity for the joint bricks, causing inflammation and disrupting function.

Arthritis Induced by Chemicals

Is there any evidence or substantiation that chemicals can cause arthritis?

One serious type of arthritis, systemic lupus erythematosus (SLE), closely related to rheumatoid arthritis, has been induced by several drugs. Remember that drugs are chemicals. One of these chemicals is hydralazine (its trade name is Apresolin,) which is used in the treatment of high blood pressure, and there is evidence that this drug has caused this devastating form of arthritis.

Procainamid, another medication used to control abnormal heartbeat rhythm, has also been shown to have caused the same disease. And phenothiazines, a major group of tranquilizers, have been responsible for numerous cases of SLE.

Other medications, such as various antibiotics, have also induced systemic lupus erythematosus and probably other types of arthritis. The mere removal of these chemicals has spectacularly "cured" this type of induced disease. These facts are known to the medical profession. It is the direct "cause-effect-cure" syndrome: A poisonous chemical was ingested—*causing* a pathological condition in the joint bricks—*effecting* a condition called arthritis—and *cured* by not taking any more of the hydralazine, procainamid, or whatever chemical the arthritis victim had ingested.

Another example of chemical poisoning resulting in symptoms highly resembling a typical case of arthritis was reported by Dr. Gerald T. Perkoff, professor of medicine at Washington University, St. Louis, Missouri. His report said: "The changes in the muscles of alcoholics pass through several stages, first there are chemical alterations, then tenderness, then increasingly severe muscle cramps, then a wasting away of the muscle tissue, and finally weakness that is often severe enough to incapacitate the alcoholic totally. It appears more than likely that the alcohol itself is poisonous to the muscle cells."

Dr. Perkoff went on to say: "In the chemical changes the muscle cells lose large amounts of vital protein called myoglobin, which normally serves to carry oxygen into the muscle tissue. Under the electron microscope the leaking muscle cells separate into weakened fibers, and also show dangerous swellings. When the muscle disease comes on suddenly, it goes just as fast—after a few days or weeks in a hospital with no alcohol and good nutrition. But it will come back if the patient starts drinking again. Patients whose muscle disease has persisted for a long time, however, are much harder to treat; it may take months before their strength returns."

Here again is a "cause-effect-cure" syndrome.

Put in my terms, when the poisonous alcohol injured the muscle bricks, it caused the loss of a large amount of myoglobin. As a result, the victim started to have severe muscle cramps due to oxygen deficiency. Under the electronic microscope Dr. Perkoff saw that the leaking muscle bricks were broken into pieces and the whole structure began to swell. When the patient is confined in a hospital and prevented from putting the poison into his body, the trillions of muscle bricks regenerate themselves and he recovers. But let this person ingest the poison again, and this same symptom complex recurs.

This experiment by Dr. Perkoff is vital because there are other very serious forms of arthritis called polymyalgia rheumatica, polymyositis, and dermatomyositis, whose symptoms are very similar to those he studied.

Let us consider this case history from my own files. *[Mrs. A. P., a 50-year-old office worker from San Francisco, came into my office complaining of pains in both of her shoulders and hips. These pains radiated down both arms and both legs. Mrs. P. had been treated by her own personal physician and also by a specialist. They gave her a series of tests and diagnosed her problem as polymyositis.]*

"This trouble started in July, 1973, and I first thought I had the flu because I had pains in all my joints and muscles. I took some aspirins and after two days the pains went away. But soon afterward the pains came back—only worse than before. They were in my shoulders, arms, legs, thighs, the tips of my fingers and the tips of my toes. I felt like I was paralyzed.

"In the mornings, I had the feeling that I had been poisoned and felt unusually fatigued. The doctors had given me pills to take and I was not getting any better. I was vomiting and feeling worse each day. I was failing instead of being helped.

[Mrs. A. P. was sent to me by one of my patients. She was put on the Dong Diet. The patient had been taking approximately 15 aspirins a day and 5 mgs. of Valium twice a day for her nervousness. As the aspirins did not seem to relieve her pains, I prescribed Darvon (65 mgs.) three times a day. She was told to continue with the Valium.]

"After only a week I began to feel better and now two months later, all the pains are gone. I have not felt like this since I was 18 years old. I have been strictly on the diet—no fooling around or cheating. I have fish with all my meals, even in the morning before I go to work. I bought a *wok* and cook Chinese-style food. I do not want any more of these pains, so I am following the diet absolutely."

[Mrs. A. P. does not take any medication at the present time.]

In the *Primer on the Rheumatic Diseases,* compiled by the Arthritis Foundation, polymyositis and dermatomyositis are defined as "diffused inflammatory disorders of striated muscle . . . these are perplexing disorders of unknown cause, which occur in all age groups, and are usually grouped with the connective tissue diseases . . . the classical rash of dermatomyositis occurs in about 40% of patients with inflammatory myopathy."

Polymyositis, then, is an inflammation of many muscles of the body—and dermatomyositis is the same disease, inflammation of the muscles, accompanied by dermatitis, or skin rash, in about 40 percent of the cases.

I do not know what poisonous substances or how much Mrs. A. P. might have ingested, but whatever they were, the allergens were in her food and they created the same onset of symptoms as Dr. Perkoff's alcoholic—aches, pains, and stiffness. Her doctors had diagnosed her condition as polymyositis, on symptoms and laboratory tests. Such tests show an excess of muscle enzymes in the blood, that can be detected and measured and which indicated muscle destruction. Trillions of her muscle bricks, then, were insulted, damaged, and destroyed.

In polymyositis, the toxic substance carried by the blood vessels attack only the muscle bricks, breaking them to pieces and causing the inflammation. But in dermatomyositis, in addition to attacking the muscle bricks, some of the poison goes into the skin bricks causing severe inflammation of the skin, or dermatitis. Now you may ask: Why doesn't the poison attack everyone in the same way? The answer is that human beings are unique—no two individuals are alike, no two fingerprints are alike, no two sets of teeth are alike. Therefore, when people are poisoned, there are qualitative and quantitative differences due to the strength and natural resistance of each brick or group of bricks.

Two Typical Cases of Arthritis Treated by My Diet

Mrs. C. C., age seventy-five, gave me the following story on her first visit to my office on March 7, 1974. She was already on the Dong Diet which she had learned about through my book.

"I had been suffering with arthritic pains in my shoulders, back, neck and hips for approximately five years. I was treated at one of the large hospital clinics by several doctors. The pain seemed to be the most severe in both of my hips, and the only relief that I got was going to the hospital to get Novocain shots to quell the pains. The attacks would vary from one to three months and in between times I just toughed it out. When the pains became too unbearable, my son would put me in a wheelchair and take me to the hospital to get these shots.

"About three years ago I was not satisfied with all these shots and not getting any better. So I went to a private rheumatologist. After much examination, he diagnosed my arthritis as progressive osteoarthritis. He said there was no hope for a cure. It came with old age. Taking aspirin was all he said that I should do as the other drugs were too strong for me at my age. I continued with this doctor until I heard about the diet.

"Within a couple of weeks—that seems such a short time now, but I am sure that it was just that—I started to get relief from the pains. And after a couple of months, I was experiencing a return of youthful strength in spite of my age. By January I would have flashes of strength that I would just sit and enjoy, it was so wonderful. It was just like a burst of sunshine through the clouds. Just youthful energy. I have not been in a wheelchair since going on the diet. I just get a twinge of pain here and there once in a while that shows me that I may have veered away from the diet a little. Then I search within myself to see what I might have eaten that was wrong. Eliminating that particular food would then clear up the pains."

Mr. P. E. of Rhinebeck, N.Y., the second case, also learned of the diet through my book, and wrote me the details on September 13, 1974.

"It was just a year ago that the pain, swelling, and stiffness in my ankles and feet was so bad that I would be awake in tears at night. Actually the problem of aching feet started in May, 1973; by September I was on crutches, unable to walk. I went to see a local orthopedic specialist who felt the problem was rheumatoid arthritis and suggested I see an internist to make certain that there was nothing else causing the pain. The internist concurred with the rheumatoid arthritis diagnosis but sent me to a rheumatologist for further examination. I was placed on a regimen of

20–25 Ecotrin (spare the stomach and good-bye intestines!) and a cortisone derivative daily. After a few weeks of continuing pain, I entered University Hospital in New York City for a month of exhaustive testing and bed rest (and more Ecotrin).

"After being discharged I walked about ten city blocks to have a prescription for orthopedic shoes filled, and by the time I arrived there I felt like I had before I went to the hospital.

"I stayed in contact with the internist by telephone and he altered the medication dosages (kind of like roulette), but to no avail. After three more weeks of worsening pain, along with a bonus of muted hearing, dizziness, and hot flashes, I heard of *The Arthritic's Cookbook,* which I purchased at a nearby book shop. As per instructions, I threw away the pills, went on the diet, and thanks to the loving care and attention of my wife, and the diet (to which she also adheres), I am now completely relieved of all pain and discomfort. I'm on my feet 12 to 14 hours daily with no problems whatsoever. I'm forty years old, but my body feels like it did when I was twenty."

Commentary on the Above Two Cases

Mrs. C. C.'s 60 trillion bricks were hale, healthy, and sound for seventy years before the toxic substances were able to attack them, causing her to have what was diagnosed as "hopeless progressive osteoarthritis." She was given the usual large doses of aspirin, and injections to help her pains. But none of her doctors attempted to look for the cause of the disease. Consequently, the poisons that originally caused her condition, together with the large doses of aspirin, without doubt continued more and more to attack her joint bricks, causing her to be confined to a wheelchair.

When Mrs. C. followed my diet, she had an almost immediate recovery, and she is now in good health. Even at seventy-five years of age, when the poisons were removed, her trillions of bricks were able to regenerate, so that Mrs. C. was able to have "flashes of strength" and to be "full of youthful energy."

In the second case, Mr. P. E. was diagnosed as having rheumatoid arthritis. His several doctors had followed the usual procedure of giving him large doses of Ecotrin (aspirin) and also a cortisone derivative. His condition became worse, and here we have the identical circumstances as Mrs. C.'s case. The original poison plus large doses of aspirin damaged trillions of the bricks in his body, making it impossible for him to walk. When he followed my diet, these bricks regenerated, and he was relieved of all his pain and discomfort.

These two cases are typical of the many arthritis cases that have had remarkable remissions after being on my diet. Their recovery seems dramatic and almost unbelievable after what they went through with the usual orthodox treatment. To be sure, not all rheumatic disease cases will get dramatic relief merely by following the diet alone, because their cases may be complicated by other diseases. For this reason, I advise everyone who has arthritis to have a complete physical examination periodically.

4

The Relation of Food Allergy to Arthritis

Allergy to food has been known for thousands of years. In the year 3000 B.C., Shen Nung, China's first emperor, and his physicians observed that some people after eating certain types of seafood developed hives, which the Chinese people called *fung non*. They described this as an itching skin disease that produced red blotches or welts and occurred either in local areas of the body or was generalized. Other symptons associated with the disease were vomiting, diarrhea, dizziness, and difficulty in breathing. As a result, Shen Nung decreed that all pregnant women in China must stop eating seafood. He reasoned that the "poison" that caused *fung non* might cause miscarriages and possibly other disorders.

Egyptians, too, knew of the ailments created by allergy, for the symptons are chronicled on their tablets and on the walls of their tombs.

And Lucretius, a Roman poet and part-time physician who lived during the first century B.C., has been credited with the adage, "One man's meat is another man's poison." Early doctors were baffled by manifestations of diseases brought on by food—for why should one person be able to eat meat and feel well, while another person becomes ill on the same fare?

In the Old Testament dietary restrictions were outlined because through observation and experience certain foods were noted to create physical disorders.

Statistics on Allergic Diseases Today

Authorities say that in the United States there are approximately 100 million people who have some sort of allergy—to the air that they breathe, which causes sneezing or asthma, to what they eat or drink, which causes stomachaches or diarrhea, or to things that they touch, which gives them a skin reaction. This is what we call allergy—a person is allergic to those various items that make him ill.

Industry loses 200 million days of work annually because workers are sick with allergy-related diseases; the medical and drug costs are approximately $300 million yearly. Because of occupational skin disorders, another 750,000 people do not report to work. Allergy is the most common chronic disease of childhood. Possibly 15 million children have allergic problems that should be treated by physicians, but only one-third of them receive any medical care.

Allergy is a serious, crippling, and fatal disease in children. It accounts for millions of school days lost annually. Asthma alone causes more death in children than any other disease, except tuberculosis. Among adults it is estimated that there are 10 million suffering from asthma—and that there are 10,000 deaths resulting from it yearly.

But the American public as a whole has not been very concerned with allergy because compared to other diseases, allergic diseases cause few deaths—they only make life miserable and debilitating. Only people who are afflicted with allergies or have children with allergic diseases are greatly concerned.

Our great achievements in science have only increased allergens—the substances that cause allergic diseases—a hundredfold. For instance, smog, a mixture of fog and pollutants from industrial waste and automobiles, has made cities hazardous to live in. In Los Angeles the atmosphere is so polluted that physicians recommend that the elderly and people with respiratory diseases move out of the city if possible.

Obviously, anything that can help solve the problems of allergy will be of great value, and it is most important to emphasize the science of allergy in the training of our future doctors.

Allergy and the Medical Profession

However, the science of allergy, like the science of nutrition, is not taught in many medical schools. In fact, a survey of seventy medical schools indicated that 95 percent of them gave very little, if any, training in the subject of allergy. This is why it is often said that allergy is the stepchild of medicine.

The emphasis in medical schools today is bacteriologically oriented. As a result, many doctors, when confronted with a disease not related to microbial agents, are puzzled. For example, hospital charts will frequently read: "migraine headaches, unknown origin"; "polyneuritis, unknown origin"; "bursitis, unknown origin." In my opinion, many such diseases of unknown origin could be allergy-related, and my clinical experience shows that 75 percent of these types of cases respond to dietary measures.

Specific Examples of Diseases Caused by Allergy to Food

Dr. William Philpott, a research director at the Fuller Memorial Hospital in South Attleboro, Massachusetts, in an article in the San Francisco *Examiner*, said: "What is now being diagnosed as schizophrenia may in fact be no more than an allergy." He believes that it is an allergic reaction, resulting in the swelling of the patient's brain, that causes the mental disorder.

Dr. Philpott thinks that approximately 80 percent of mankind suffers from allergic reactions and that the reactions are not always as obvious as when one breaks out in hives after eating strawberries.

The article further stated: "Dr. Philpott said 92%

of the patients he examined reacted to something. . . .
Wheat was the most common irritant, causing reactions in 64%; followed by corn 51%; and milk 50%.
The average patient reacted to ten things. No patient reacted to just one."

The distinguished allergist, Dr. Ben F. Feingold, chief emeritus of the allergy department of the Kaiser Foundation Hospital in San Francisco, in his studies of hyperkinetic children—children with behavior disturbances and learning difficulties—tells of cases of wall climbing, head knocking, and uncontrollable impulsiveness. He cites a case of a seven-year-old child who was so aggressive that he would charge at automobiles while riding on his bicycle. Although many of the children were of normal or high IQ, they had learning difficulties because they manifested such impetuousness that they could not get the words out of their mouths and they were unable to sit still long enough to concentrate on their schoolwork. Dr. Feingold found that artificial flavors and colors, some vitamins, hot dogs, and such ordinary foods as apples, peaches, apricots, cucumbers, tomatoes, and all berries can cause hyperactivity in these children.

When the children were put on a special diet, these conditions cleared up completely. Dr. Feingold said: "Children on medication with behavior-modifying drugs such as amphetamines, methylphenidates, tranquilizers and antidepressants were able to discontinue the drugs, even with a history of many years of such therapy."

Dr. Marguerite Stemmerman, A West Virginia internist at the Owen Institute of Nervous and Mental Disorders, reported a case of a one-year-old child with multiple petit mal seizures. She found they were due to the additive MSG (monosodium glutamate). In three days, after MSG was deleted from the child's diet, the attacks stopped dramatically, and while on the MSG-free diet, the child was free of all seizures. In an experiment one year later, the child was given one-half of a frankfurter containing MSG, and within three hours the seizures of petit mal again recurred.

Since then, the child has stayed on the MSG-free diet and has enjoyed good health without incident.

In 1972, Dr. Jean Mayer, professor of nutrition at Harvard University, reported a case of a ten-year-old boy who died from an allergic reaction to eating peanuts.

Recent reports indicate that nearly 4,000 people in the United States die from choking to death because of food obstructions every year. These attacks which occur frequently in restaurants, are often mistaken for heart attacks and thus have become known as "café coronaries." Without doubt, a large number of these incidents are similar to what happened to the 10-year-old boy. In medical terminology this is called an angioedema of the larynx, which means asphyxiation due to the swelling of the throat caused by an allergic reaction to food and food additives.

Drs. J. A. Rudolph and D. M. Rudolph, both specialists in allergy at the University of Miami School of Medicine, said in their excellent book *Allergies— What They Are and What to Do about Them*: ". . . recent studies have revealed that such illnesses as rheumatic fever, rheumatoid arthritis, scleroderma, dermatomyositis, and certain forms of nephritis, anemias and blood and blood vessel diseases resemble hypersensitivity reactions which have been produced in the laboratory."

Dr. Howard G. Rapaport and Shirley Motter Linde, M.S., in *The Complete Allergy Guide,* state: ". . . one patient had no problem with milk when she was a child, but in later life developed severe sensitivity reaction to it. Every day she drank milk for breakfast, and about two hours later, she had diarrhea—two days later the joints of her arms and legs became tender and swollen . . . by watching her diet she has not had any attacks."

They report another case of a ". . . woman who had suffered with asthma for 28 years. Nothing seemed to help . . . it was discovered that she was sensitive to milk. A quarter of a century of misery from asthma was ended as soon as she eliminated milk and milk products from her diet."

Evidence of Diseases Caused by Allergy Largely Ignored

From the above discussion you can see that many millions of people are suffering from allergic diseases that can create alarming physical and mental disabilities. It would appear that the combination of a relative abundance of food and bad eating habits has led to a whole spectrum of diseases—heart diseases, kidney disorders, lung ailments, hypertension, diabetes, obesity, strokes, and even mental disorders—in which nutritional factors are either the main cause or highly contributory.

With the increasing clinical evidence of degenerative diseases being caused by food allergies, I cannot understand how the medical profession can still ignore the study of allergy and nutrition.

Rheumatic Diseases Caused by Allergy

Allergists are the only group of physicians with the courage to postulate that the cause of rheumatic diseases is allergy. Their theory is that rheumatoid arthritis is caused by a form of allergy called autoimmunity, a phenomenon in which the body's defense system goes awry—and turns against the body's own tissues. Ordinarily, the defense system of the body only manufactures antibodies against foreign substances such as disease germs, viruses, and chemicals. The body has a built-in mechanism to prevent its defense system from attacking its own tissues.

According to *The Complete Allergy Guide*, "No one really knows what brings about the appearance of these self-destroying antibodies known as autoantibodies. Scientists don't know whether it is a result of aging, injury, the action of enzymes or even the action of viruses or bacteria.

"No matter what the orgin of these autoantibodies, the results are devastating as the body attacks its own tissues. The autoimmune processes occur in a wide variety of places; in the gastrointestinal tract, in the muscles, the joints, the blood, the nervous system, the glands, the eyes.

"Every year physicians attribute more and more diseases to the autoimmmune reactions. They include arthritis . . . and systemic lupus erythematosus."

Let me take you to my Fantasyland once more to try to explain autoimmunity in a different way.

City of Fantasia

In this city there is a huge manufacturing plant that produces solid-gold replicas of the human body. A force of 20,000 workers is employed on a twenty-four-hour basis, for there is a great demand for this unusual product throughout the world.

To protect this large complex the management imported 2,000 giant panda bears from Tibet. These beautiful animals are world-renowned for their ability to guard large buildings. Their intelligence equals that of a human being, and in addition, they have an unfailing instinct that enables them to distinguish between employees and outsiders, even at night. They never make a mistake between friend or foe.

However, these giant panda bears have one quirk. When they attack anyone, they bite only their joints—the ankles, knees, hips, elbows, and shoulders.

For many years there were no burglaries because everyone was aware that these giant panda guards were on duty. Through lack of excitement and because they were well-fed—always in a royal manner with the American well-balanced diet—the animals soon became fat and lazy. Then for no apparent reason, a group of them started to attack many of the employees of the plant just as if they were outsiders. These pandas were immediately isolated, and local doctors tried to treat them, but to no avail. Finally, famous specialists from all over the world were called in.

It is said that $15 million a year was spent in trying

to find the cause of what they called the autoimmune disease that made the giant pandas lose their fine instinct to differentiate between employees and outsiders. In the meantime, the only medication recommended by the famous specialists was large doses of aspirin. For those who did not respond to the aspirin, stronger medications such as Butazolidin, Indocin, antimalarial drugs, and cortisone were used. Many of the panda bears were also given injections—not the ordinary kind, but gold shots. For the few animals that did not respond to any of the above treatments, cytotoxic drugs (used in the treatment of cancer) were administered. All these drugs were used to treat the symptoms of the panda disease, but they did not cure it.

The scientists' failure to find the cause of the disease after spending so much time and money created much dissatisfaction. Some critics contended that because the scientists were trained to believe that all panda diseases were caused by bacteria or viruses, they had spent all their research money in that direction—and they had produced no results. Yet there was overwhelming evidence that panda diseases could also be caused by nutritional factors. Angered by this criticism, the specialists retaliated by making this blanket statement: "The relationship between diet and panda disease has been thoroughly and scientifically studied. The simple proven fact is: no food has anything to do with causing panda disease and no food is effective in treating or curing it."

One critic, out of curiosity, went to the famous University of California medical library and searched through twenty years of the *Index Medicus* but could not find a single written scientific document to prove that statement.

Another critic theorized that since these beautiful animals were from Tibet, feeding them the luxurious American well-balanced diet "poisoned" the area of their brains that controls their instinct, thus causing the panda disease.

The evidence to support this was in Dr. Feingold's experiments with hyperkinetic children; Dr. Stemmerman's MSG-free diet for the one-year-old child with petit mal seizures, and the work of Dr. Philpott, who believed that allergy to foods caused mental disorders.

But the great scientists continued to look for that mysterious virus. And this, in effect, is the situation today in the city of Fantasia.

Food Allergens as the Cause of Arthritis
—My Hypothesis

I want to repeat here what Dr. Howard G. Rapaport said: "No one really knows what brings about the appearance of these self-destroying antibodies known as autoantibodies. Scientists don't know whether it is a result of aging, injury, the action of enzymes or even the action of viruses or bacteria."

In other words, the key question to this whole puzzle is: What *triggers* the whole reaction, or what is the *inciting agent* that starts the entire process of antibodies attacking their own tissues? (Or what caused the panda bears to lose their instinct to differentiate between employees and outsiders and start biting the employees?)

Most rheumatologists still believe that a virus started the whole event and then disappeared. They have spent years in search of that mysterious parasite, but up to this moment, none has been discovered.

My hypothesis as to the cause of arthritis is that the *inciting factors* are food allergens—and food allergens, in my estimation, may be considered a "poison." Think again of the definition in *Dorland's Medical Dictionary*: "poison—any substance which when ingested, or developed within the body in relatively small amounts, by its chemical action may cause damage to structure or disturbance of function."

In the next few pages I want to give some more of my clinical cases to support my contention—and I'll leave the results for you to evaluate. Again, these cases are not given in the usual formal manner. Each of them was tape-recorded, so the patients could tell their stories as they wished.

NAME:	Mr. I. Z.
AGE:	71
RESIDENCE:	California
OCCUPATION:	Jewelry salesman
DIAGNOSIS:	Osteoarthritis of the spine
DURATION:	Since 1952
FIRST VISIT:	April 19, 1973
PREVIOUS MEDICATION:	Aspirin, Indocin, Butazolidin, steroids
INTERVIEWED:	August 8, 1974

"It was July, 1952, and I was walking down the street, when I had a strong pain in my ribs. It extended from my back around to my chest. I took a few steps and then rested on a fire hydrant for about 20 minutes. When I felt better, I walked back to my jewelry store, which was about a block away. Every time I put my foot down it felt like a shock. It was very painful. The pain went from my foot straight up to my chest. At that time I was fifty years old.

"I called the local Medical Association, and I asked them to help me. They gave me five or six doctors' names. I picked one out and called him. The first thing he asked me over the phone was if I had the money to pay for the office visit. That made me mad. So I hung up and called another doctor. The second doctor sent me to a hospital for x-rays, mylograms and all kinds of examinations. He gave me a rainbow of pills to take and lots of shots. Nothing happened. I still had the pains. After two months of this kind of treatment, the doctor wanted to give me more of the same, so I walked out.

"I travel a lot up and down the Coast because I am a jewelry salesman. Whenever one of my friends in various towns recommended his doctor, I would go to

him to see if I could get some relief from all my pain.
I had also been to all kinds of physio-therapists. They
gave me hot baths, cold baths, hot sand on my back
and shoulders. I would get relief for a few hours and
then the pain would come back again. In other words,
I was getting no results—I felt I was throwing my
money away.

"I decided to go to the Mayo Clinic because my sister
had been there and had liked it. So I went there with
my problems and spent a week. They said that I had
osteoarthritis, a kind of disease that there is no cure
for. I was very discouraged, but I had to go from one
doctor to another trying to get relief from the pains
that I had. I finally went to the Veterans Hospital. I
was there six times. They also told me that there was
no cure for my kind of back trouble. All they gave me
was pain tablets.

[*The case history of 72-year-old Mr. I. Z. exempli-
fies the "treatment mentality" of most of today's physicians. "Osteoarthritis is tantamount to instant old
age. We can't do anything about the process of aging,
so just take aspirin the rest of your golden days." I
started him on the diet and gradually had him cut
down on the medication he was taking.*]

"For the first couple of months, I did not seem to
get results, but the pains were disappearing gradually.
Then, after six months, I threw away all the colored
pills that I had been getting from all the other doctors.
I am not taking any tablets at all now. In fact, about
a year ago, I bought some arthritis pain tablets, and I
still have 75 of the 100 tablets. My wife takes one
once in a while. But I do not take them any more.

"I work in the garden, I walk and ride in my car
without any pain. In fact, I just came back from Miami last week. I am entirely a different person now. I
weighed 171 pounds a year ago and now I weigh 154
pounds. I feel like a young man. I feel like I had two
lives—one that I had with pains for 20 years, and one
that I have now without pain."

[Mr. I. Z. responded to my treatment program so well that he recently returned from an exploration trip to the Antarctic to study the sex life of the penguins.]

NAME:	Mrs. P. S.
AGE:	28
RESIDENCE:	Colorado
OCCUPATION:	Housewife
DIAGNOSIS:	Rheumatoid arthritis
DURATION:	Two and one-half years
PREVIOUS MEDICATION:	20 aspirin a day, prednisone orally, Indocin, Butazolidin alka, Naproxen (a new drug that is dispensed only by selected rheumatologists for clinical use, before being approved for general use)
FIRST VISIT:	August 16, 1974
INTERVIEWED:	August 16, 1974

"About two and one-half years ago, one month after the birth of my child, I found myself extremely fatigued. I began to feel stiffness and pain in my joints, especially in the morning. At first I thought it was simply the after effects of my pregnancy. However, soon my joints started to swell, first in my fingers, then in my wrists and shoulders, and finally down to my knees. After completing a series of laboratory tests and x-ray examinations, the doctors told me that the laboratory tests showed that I had rheumatoid arthritis. I was seriously ill for a whole year. I could not bathe myself, or dress myself, or hold my new baby. I could hardly walk.

"I was taking 20 aspirin a day, and also, subsequently, cortisone, Indocin, and Butazolidin alka by mouth. The medicine also made me very ill. I had been taking gold shots too. But nothing seemed to help me, and I got worse and worse. Both of my knees became terribly inflamed and swollen. They became about twice the size of normal knees, and naturally, I could not walk at all then.

"The rheumatologist said that if I did not get better I would have to have them drained. That was what I should expect from the disease, rheumatoid arthritis. The doctor made an appointment for me with the hospital to have the knees drained in two weeks.

"In the meantime, I found *The Arthritic's Cookbook*. I went on the diet. When I went back to the rheumatologist in two weeks, my knees were back down to normal size. He could not believe this at all. He said that he had not seen anything like this in his life.

[This case is almost a classical textbook picture of rheumatoid arthritis. The American Rheumatism Association has developed clinical criteria for the diagnosis of this disease. The patient had morning stiffness and pain at the beginning of her illness. And in addition, there was swelling in the joints of her hands, wrists, and shoulders on both sides. Later both knees became swollen with fluid which her doctor planned to drain. These signs and symptoms are almost exactly as listed in the clinical criteria. Her doctor's laboratory tests confirmed the diagnosis. In addition this disease affects women three times more frequently than men, and the age bracket is usually young adults under the age of forty.

The patient was given the usual treatment by her doctors, which began with large doses of aspirin and subsequently Indocin, Butazolidin alka, and cortisone. Because she did not respond well with oral medication, she was also given gold therapy.

The patient came into my office on August 16, 1974, for one consultation. Since she had already decreased the amount of drug medication herself after her relief by adhering to the Dong Diet, I advised her to continue the Naproxen and one prednisone a day. Naproxen is a new drug that is not yet available for general use in the United States. It is used mainly as a drug designed to relieve both pain and inflammation. Its side effects are said to be less than those of aspirin.]

"I do not take any more aspirin. I do not take anything now but a Naproxen, and one prednisone a day.

"I do not have any pains any more, and just a little stiffness once in a while. I am not tired any more during the day like I used to be."

NAME:	Mrs. L. De W.
AGE:	67
RESIDENCE:	California
OCCUPATION:	Retired secretary
DIAGNOSIS:	Rheumatoid arthritis
DURATION:	28 years
PREVIOUS MEDICATION:	16 aspirins a day, Darvon 2 times a day, gold therapy, steroid injections when pain is severe, Butazoldin and Butazoldin alka once a day
FIRST VISIT:	January 31, 1974
INTERVIEWED:	January 31, 1974

"I have had rheumatoid arthritis since I was 39 years old. By taking large doses of aspirin and gold shots, I had been able to work until I was 64 years of age. Then I retired. I had been taking gold shots, 16 aspirins a day, Darvon two times a day, Butazolidin once a day, and if the pain became too severe, I would take a cortisone shot. I also had been taking Valium in order to sleep.

"My condition had become so bad that I ached in every part of my body, but especially in my thumbs. I also had spurs on my feet and found it difficult to stand for any length of time.

"I heard about *The Arthritic's Cookbook* and purchased a copy. When I went to see my doctor about four months ago, I asked him if he knew about the diet. I had brought my copy of the book to his office for him to see. He said, 'Oh, I know about the diet, and I have read the book. My wife bought it. I don't think it would help you, but you can try it.'

"Now, three and one-half months later, I can drive my car. I can hold a pen and write again. I can dance and I am full of pep. I feel great all over. I can take baths now, because I can lower myself into the tub, where I was not able to before. I could not dress myself, or comb my own hair, or even turn the doorknob to get in or out of a room. Now I can do all those things. I could not wash my neck because I could not get my hands and arms around to do this. . . . I am so happy to be able to do these things now.

"I had a thyroid nodule that interfered with my swallowing once in awhile; now this has disappeared. My doctor is amazed with my progress. The last time that he examined me he said that I was in better health now than I have been since I first came to see him. I asked him if I should continue on with Dr. Dong's Diet, and he said, 'By all means, do not go off it at all!' "

NAME:	Mrs. N. C.
AGE:	63
RESIDENCE:	Idaho
OCCUPATION:	Housewife
DIAGNOSIS:	Rheumatoid arthritis with concomitant osteoarthritis
DURATION:	4 years
PREVIOUS MEDICATION:	Aspirin, Indocin, steroid injections, steroids orally
FIRST VISIT:	August 12, 1974
INTERVIEWED:	August 16, 1974

"I have had arthritis for the past four years. It started in my right elbow and migrated down to both knees in 1972. The right knee was bad, and became increasingly worse. It was so severe that I could hardly walk. I first went to a hosptial. After a series of examinations, the doctor stated that I had rheumatoid arthritis and that nothing could be done for me. He suggested that I take aspirin for the pains.

"Then I went to see another specialist. All last summer both of my knees were so swollen that I had to put hot packs on them, even during the worst heat of the summer. I could not get up from my bed unless I put these hot packs on my knees.

"After another series of examinations, this new doctor said that I had osteoarthritis, so he gave me several shots of cortisone in the knees. The injections gave me a little relief from the pain, but the swelling did not go down at all.

"Dr. Dong's book was recommended to me by a friend. I was in the hospital at the time, and when I went home, I followed the diet quite closely. Although I disliked fish before I began the diet, I ate it. Doing without dairy products didn't bother me either, because it was worth it to get better. I began to feel a lot better and improved continously. I lost some of the stiffness, and the swelling in both my knees began to go down. I weighed about 160 pounds, and I lost 15 pounds on the diet. This helped me quite a bit.

"The best thing was that I had lots of steps in my home, and I could not manage them before. Now I go up and down with no trouble."

NAME:	Mrs. B. R.
AGE:	70
RESIDENCE:	California
OCCUPATION:	Retired employee of telephone company
DIAGNOSIS:	Rheumatoid arthritis, generalized, involving both hands, elbows, shoulders, knees, and both feet
DURATION:	4 years
PREVIOUS MEDICATION:	Prednisone, Indocin, aspirins
FIRST VISIT:	November 30, 1972
INTERVIEWED:	August 13, 1974

"In 1969 I retired from the telephone company. The first symptoms of my arthritis started in my hands a few months before I retired. I was able to use the computer and the other office equipment, but my hands would pain me, on and off. During the next two years the disease got worse and spread to other parts of my body. I live on the second floor of an apartment building, and it was very hard to get up the stairs and down them again. I had to grasp the sides of the banister to pull myself up. The doctor was giving me aspirin at first, and added Indocin later on. Then he gave me prednisone when the pain persisted and I was not able to stand it any more. All these medicines did not seem to help me very much. They relieved me at times, when I took large doses. I had pains all day long and at night I would have to get out of bed and sit in a chair when the pains in my shoulders were bad. I was only able to walk one or two blocks before the pains became too severe to continue on. I could not drive my car, because every time I would have to step on the brakes, I could barely stand the pains. If this condition had continued any longer I know that I would have had to enter a convalescent home. I would have lost my independence.

[Mrs. B. R. was put on the Dong Diet. Her medication was continued as prescribed by her previous doctor, but was gradually reduced as she improved. Now the patient takes an occasional Indocin capsule, or prednisone, whenever she shows any symptoms of pains. She has been asked to return for checkup examination in six months.]

"Now I am able to walk up and down the stairs in my apartment building without pains. I have been able to sleep all night lying down instead of sitting up in a chair. I have just returned from a Caribbean cruise and have a few pains now. Perhaps something in the vacation diet has bothered me; but, I am 70 years old now and I expect a few pains now and then. How-

ever, I can drive my car now and do my own housework. I just cannot believe that I am feeling this well."

There is a great deal of basic research going on in
the fields of allergy and nutrition. The mystifying question is why some people develop allergies while others
do not. The chemical warfare between the invading
foreign bodies and the defense system of the individual
—with the resulting reaction known as allergy—is
still unclear to medical scientists.

As practicing physicians with multitudes of patients
seeking relief from the agonies and pains of arthritis,
we must not wait for laboratory scientists to find a
definitive cure for the disease if there are other means
of giving relief and effecting remissions.

My hypothesis that rheumatic diseases are caused
by chemical poisoning and allergy to foods has accomplished these goals. As you can see from these
cases, treatments with the Dong Diet are not only effective but also dramatic. But let me repeat here again
that I am not a research scientist. To discover the biochemical facts about the relation of diet to rheumatic
diseases requires rigorous and painstaking research of
a kind that I have neither the training nor the time to
perform.

What Is the Dong Diet?

The diet that I recommend is a basic one. It includes the fundamentals of protein, vegetables, and
carbohydrates. However, there are restrictions on certain kinds of foods, which are detailed in the second
section of this book.

Two such restrictions are on milk and milk products
and fruit and fruit juices. From my years of clinical
experience, and after trial and error, I have found that
these categories of edibles, recommended by the pro-
ponents of the so-called well-balanced American diet,
are, in fact, deleterious to arthritic patients, so they
are forbidden to people on my diet.

Fruits and fruit juices have become an obsession with the American public, and millions of Americans faithfully drink juice every morning. This merely demonstrates how advertising can brainwash people.

Four-fifths of the population of the world do not eat fruit or drink fruit juices every day, either because there are no fruits in these sections or because people do not have the money to buy fruit, even when it is in season. These people survive quite well without their glass of "Florida sunshine" every morning.

Dr. Feingold reports that the elimination of certain foods, plus a diet free of artificial colorings and flavorings, can, in a matter of a few days, restore a hyperkinetic child's behavior back to normal. He said: "You can reproduce the symptoms at will, *turn them on or off,* that is the fantastic part."

In my clinical experience, I, too, have found it possible to turn symptoms on and off—"The faucet effect"—by controlling diet of patients. Those patients who eat fruit and drink milk will soon manifest symptoms of arthritis. When those items are removed from their diet, the symptoms disappear.

It is extremely important to understand that once someone goes on my diet, he or she must stay on it for the rest of his life. Many people write me saying that, now that they feel so much better, wouldn't it be all right to once in a while eat just a little fruit or just a little steak? My answer is always "no." What is the point of getting rid of the poisons in our bodies if before long we put them right back in? Even at my age and considering the length of time I have been pain-free, if I go off the diet I feel it literally within hours. Recently someone gave my family some beautiful fresh asparagus. I love asparagus but I have discovered that it is something I shouldn't eat. This time I was very much involved in this book, and in other things, and I forgot and had some for dinner. I thought back to what I might have eaten and of course realized it was the asparagus. So, strict adherence to the diet is essential, always, if one wants to remain without pain.

My diet is low in saturated fatty acids, has adequate

protein, vitamins and minerals, and carbohydrates, with all the necessary nutrients. It is a diet that eliminates all the ingredients such as high fat content in animal proteins that are the cause of many of the degenerative diseases mentioned earlier. One would think that such a diet would be very bland, but let me quote from the August, 1973, issue of *Woman's Day* magazine, whose astute young woman editor, after interviewing me about the forthcoming *Arthritic's Cookbook,* called her article: "A Special Diet for Everyone." She said: "The dishes are simply so delicious, and so suitable for almost any diet, that we offer them as good eating for everyone."

Beef, lamb, and pork are out, but don't let that alarm you. A bulletin issued by the United States Department of the Interior in September, 1961, supports the value of fish, a mainstay of my diet, as a substitute for the usual beef, lamb, or pork proteins in any diet. This bulletin states: "Fish can be consumed three times daily due to its nutritional value, and in general is applicable to any diets designed to yield (1) needed biologically valuable trace minerals; (2) high levels of vitamins, especially of the B-complex system; (3) reduction in sodium intake and consequent reduction in body water retention; (4) reduction in hard fat intake and restoration of fatty acid balance between hard and soft fats; (5) high levels of readily available, biologically complete, easily digestible proteins; and (6) increase in body energy food-intake, with maximum ease of metabolic utilization."

To those in the medical world, I have this to say: My dietary concept has given relief to thousands of arthritic victims, so it must have some therapeutic merit and value. At the very least, it should produce among medical scientists of integrity the desire to seek substantiation. In light of the millions who suffer from arthritis, it does not seem right that any possibility of helping them should be rejected out of hand.

I suggest that doctors use my dietary concept as they have been using aspirin, *empirically,* until the mechanism of why it works is substantiated. For the Dong Diet of fish, chicken, vegetables, and simple carbohydrates cannot, by any stretch of the imagination, harm any patient.

My dietary approach in the therapy of rheumatic diseases, as suggested in this book, places in doctors' hands a tool of the utmost importance. It is an addition to their specialized knowledge and an indispensable adjunct to their modes of treatment. I know that the more creative and secure among them will approach this nutritional and biochemical therapy with an open mind.

5

Exercise and the Arthritic

"Every adult should find time in his daily schedule for some form of physical activity," says the President's Council on Physical Fitness. "Medical evidence tells us that our hearts, lungs, muscles, and even our minds need the effects of regular vigorous exercise."

The majority of the people in the world seem to get along without special programs of exercise. For the people in the state of Hunza in Pakistan and the Vilcabambians, high in the Andes Mountains, for instance, climbing the terraces daily where they plant and harvest enough food for their existence is exercise.

Most Americans start exercise programs in kindergarten and many continue on through high school and college, but if they enter the world of commerce, only a few of them find time to exercise regularly before or after a day of hard work.

White-collar workers, in their sedentary jobs, do little exercising until the weekends. Most blue-collar workers use their muscles in performing their jobs so are constantly exercising. For many housewives, their household chores and gardening constitute sufficient physical activity—although it may not be what the President's Council on Physical Fitness considers "regular vigorous exercise."

What Is Exercise?

Exercise advocates, who jog for miles, play lively games of tennis, and engage in other strenuous physical activities have one concept of exercise. They feel vigorous physical exertion is beneficial for one's health.

My concept of exercise for the arthritic patient is the performance of mild physical exertion to correct physical deformities. But before therapeutic exercises can begin, the pain, muscle spasms, and joint inflammation must be relieved.

The arthritic's only desire is to be able to get out of bed in the morning, to be able to take a bath, to be able to raise his arms to comb his hair, to be able to get in and out of a chair—and someday to be able to to drive his own automobile again, so that he can be self-reliant. These simple functions of life are the "exercises" that the arthritic would like to accomplish.

When Can an Arthritic Start Exercising

My first objective with rheumatic disease patients is to free them of their pain. It has been my clinical experience over a period of years that the Dong Diet, with a moderate amount of proper medication, will usually accomplish this purpose.

As I see each patient recovering gradually from the ravages of this tragic disease, I am reminded of how fortunate I am to have recuperated myself. Just recently, a thirty-year-old former airline hostess, with a four-year history of rheumatoid arthritis, came to my office and exclaimed, "I've only seen you a few times, but last week I went shopping without my cane." A seventy-four-year-old golfer, with arthritis that had affected his shoulders, neck, and back for several years, told me enthusiastically that he was now able to play nine holes of golf without pain. And a sixty-seven-year-old housewife from Carmel, California, embraced me with tears in her eyes and said, "Doctor,

I went wading in the Pacific Ocean for the first time in ten years."

To these patients *exercise* is to be able to accomplish the *simple functions we take for granted*. That such a goal is possible is the reason I awake each morning stimulated and eager to go to my office to meet the new challenges of each "apparently hopeless" patient. I know that with my treatment methodology I can give a measure of hope, relief, and mobility to every new case. This is my elixir of life.

What Kind of Exercise Should the Arthritic Do?

My exercise rule for my arthritic patients is to be a participant, not a spectator. I advise those who are sports-minded to start their golf, tennis, or bowling again gradually—not in a competitive fashion, but only within their capacity and for the pleasure of the game. They should not exhaust themselves.

Indoor swimming in a heated pool is particularly beneficial, because the body is suspended in water and the movements put no undue strain on the joints. The contraction and stretching of the muscles in the warm water increases the circulation throughout the body which gives the patient a feeling of well-being.

Walking in the fresh air is the very best exercise that an arthritic can do, slowly or briskly, depending upon one's ability and desire. Taking a few deep breaths while walking increases the oxygen supply to the lungs, so one should remember to do this intermittently. Most areas in the United States have wonderful museums. Doing one's walking in this kind of setting is not only educational and fun but good for the arthritic as well. If the patient takes an interest in what he is doing, it does not seem like programmed exercise, and he is then more willing to participate.

Books on Exercise

More books, pamphlets, and articles have been written on exercise than on any other subject, except perhaps on sex. For those of you who would like to experiment with new and different types of exercise, look for books on kung fu, yoga, or isometrics. Try doing some of the exercises that are outlined, but use your discretion and do not exhaust yourself.

Relevant Case Histories

The August, 1974, issue of *Medical Opinion* featured on its cover a picture of a cane, a handful of capsules, some pills, a stack of hospital bills and cancelled checks. The caption was: "Low-Back Pain Syndrome, He's Crippled by Pain, 'Hooked on Medication,' Burdened by Bills."

This rather graphic description accurately fits most of my patients who have gone through years of orthodox treatment programs. The mere mention of exercise or any physical exertion terrifies most of them. But by adhering strictly to my dietary and medical plans, they are not only able to exercise but have returned to gainful work, as well.

The following case histories are relevant to this discussion:

NAME:	Mr. W. V.
AGE:	67
RESIDENCE:	California
OCCUPATION:	Retired municipal employee
DIAGNOSIS:	Rheumatoid arthritis
DURATION:	6 years
PREVIOUS MEDICATION:	Aspirin, Indocin, gold therapy
FIRST VISIT:	June 4, 1973
INTERVIEWED:	May 6, 1974

"In 1968, I was told that I had arthritis. The doctor that I went to gave me all kinds of examinations and finally said that I had rheumatoid arthritis. It began in both my hands and went down to my knees and legs on both sides.

"I was treated by my last specialist for five years. He gave me gold shots, aspirin, and everything that is usually used for this disease. Still my condition worsened every year. Both of my hands were crippled and I could hardly use them. By 1973, I was on crutches and could hardly walk—I was dragging one leg around and could not bend my knees.

[The patient was started on the diet and I told him to have his wife call me so I could give her instructions on how to cook for him.]

"I feel fine now. I walk four or five miles without any trouble. I go to my front yard and dig and spade the ground and plant things. I do not have any problems at all. I do all kinds of work around the house, and just last month I remodeled the whole kitchen. I stained the wood, put on cabinet doors, did all the plumbing and electrical work myself—getting up and down from the floor without any trouble. Nothing, nothing hurts me!

"The only time I have any aches is when I overwork and stay in the yard too long. Then I go in to have my lunch and take a siesta."

NAME:	Mrs. I. D.
AGE:	58
RESIDENCE:	California
OCCUPATION:	Housewife
DIAGNOSIS:	Rheumatoid arthritis
DURATION:	Since age 12
PREVIOUS MEDICATION:	Aspirin, steroids, "and every new kind of medicine that they could give me"
FIRST VISIT:	March 7, 1974
INTERVIEWED:	December 6, 1974

"I have had rheumatoid arthritis for many years. The pains were terrible. I could not walk, could not sleep, and my knees, shoulders, hands, neck, and all over my body ached until it was almost unbearable. Pains in my hands were so bad that I would just sit there and cry. Every time I would telephone my doctor to complain, he would just tell me to increase the aspirin tablets. Even then the pains were not alleviated and I would take a few more in the hopes of relief. My case was diagnosed by an internist as rheumatoid arthritis. Periodically I would have attacks when I would have to go back on crutches and stay in bed completely.

[Mrs. I. D. had begun the diet on her own after her daughter-in-law read about my book.]

"The pains started to let up in about a week or two, after I had begun the diet. I began to walk without pain and was not taking aspirin. Within a month even the stiffness started to leave me. I began to do all my own housework again, and the cooking also.

"When I was very ill, it was so painful to get out of my bed to go to the bathroom that I had to be helped. But as I began to get well from the diet, I could feel myself straightening up again—and my husband would say to the children, 'Doesn't your mother look wonderful again?'

"Now I am feeling so well that I am going to start taking tennis lessons soon. Yesterday I played tennis with my daughter and rallied back and forth. Every time my son looks at me, he says he cannot believe it is the same mother that was bed-ridden and in such pain."

NAME:	Mrs. S. N.
AGE:	62
RESIDENCE:	Louisiana
OCCUPATION:	Housewife
DIAGNOSIS:	Osteoarthritis of the lower spine
DURATION:	3 years (with constant pain)
PREVIOUS MEDICATION:	Aspirin, Indocin, Darvon
FIRST VISIT:	October 16, 1973
INTERVIEWED:	November 13, 1974

"I lived with terrible pains in my back for the past few years. I had a bad fall from horseback a few years ago and I never fully recovered from it. It had become increasingly worse to the point that when I sat down in the chair, I could not get out of it at all. In the mornings, I could hardly get out of bed. The pains were constant and I almost gave up in despair.

"I had been to various doctors and many specialists for different kinds of treatments, but it had done me no good. Finally I heard about Dr. Dong. With his strict diet and treatments, I can now go out and get on one of the cable cars here in San Francisco. I can run up and down the stairs and sit in chairs and be able to get out of them again. I can do all those little everyday things that I could not do before. The same is true for walking. I was not able to walk or to do any exercises before. But now in Belvedere, where I am staying with my cousin, I find myself walking over to the boardwalk and shopping. These are things that I was unable to do before."

6

Longevity: Everyone's Goal

If you are wondering what a chapter on longevity is doing in a book about arthritis, you will be surprised to learn that the Dong Diet is not only beneficial for victims of arthritis, but also has longevity as one of its significant rewards.

Dr. Ralph Nelson, chief of the Clinical Nutrition Department, Mayo Clinic, Rochester, Minnesota, said at an American Medical Association conference in 1973: *"There will someday be such a thing as a longevity diet."* The doctor goes on to describe a diet that is already here, the diet that I have been recommending for over thirty-five years. Dr. Nelson said: "It will be a diet to which very little or nothing will be added, but from which a lot of things people now customarily eat will be omitted. That the Americans eat too much is hardly news, but what is news to a lot of people is the fact that the vitamins and other supplements, extra proteins and diet additives, recommended by food faddists, not only do no good for the average person, they may do a great deal of harm. They are among the items the longevity diet will omit."

Once it has been researched and established, Dr. Nelson feels that the longevity diet will be low in calories and proteins. Today Americans are over-indulging in these food elements. He said: "Americans are shortening their lifespan by consuming too

102

much protein . . . we do not store excess protein in our bodies, but excrete it in the form of nitrogen. In very common language, the high protein diet fills our system with garbage that must be treated by the kidneys. Excess protein forces the body to work harder to get rid of that garbage."

Dr. Nelson concluded that "People who stuff themselves with high protein and high caloric foods shorten their lives. Carbohydrate loading can cause heart trouble and swallowing vitamin supplements can be poisonous."

What Is Old Age?

In the United States, when you reach sixty-five, you are supposed to be entering old age. Everything is geared for retirement—Medicare cards are issued for your hospitalization and medical insurance care; businesses large and small request your retirement, and you are given a pension. You are brainwashed into believing that your contribution to the active world of commerce and industry are terminated and that your skills and experience are no longer needed. Elsewhere in the world, chronological age is of no concern; personal skills, ability, and knowledge are appreciated indefinitely.

Sydney J. Harris, in one of his philosophical meanderings, wrote: "When I hear of men being forced to retire at 65, I think of Kant writing his 'Anthropology' at 74; Tintoretto painting his 'Paradise' at 74; Verdi composing his opera 'Otello' at 74; Goethe completing his 'Trilogy of Passion' at 74 —and Titian painting his historic 'Battle of Lepanto' at 98."

Employment should be based on a person's competence and skill, not his age. Forced retirement can seriously impair mental and physical health—the loss of prestige, loss of routine, and loss of activity all contribute to the sense of worthlessness. The nation is then forced to support the retiree and it loses his or her productivity.

What is Longevity?

Longevity, according to Webster, is "length of life." But scientists are more difinite about how long an individual will live. They estimate that all mammals should live five times the number of years it takes their skeleton to mature. Since a dog matures at three years, fifteen years is the normal life of a dog. A human being matures at twenty-five, therefore, humans should really live to be one hundred twenty-five years of age. By those standards, then, if a person does not live to be at least a hundred years old, with good health, vigor, and vitality, then he is depriving himself of many years of happy living.

What Shortens Life?

In eighteenth century America the average length of life was about thirty-five years of age. Most deaths at that time were due to infectious diseases—pneumonia, influenza, tuberculosis, enteritis, and diphtheria—because of the lack of preventive medicine and sanitation.

Since the discovery of penicillin by Sir Alexander Fleming, and the development of other antibiotics, the death rate from these diseases has been reduced. Now the average life expectancy in the United States is sixty-nine and one-half years. So we are still short of the goal by over fifty years. Noninfectious diseases such as heart disease, atherosclerosis, cerebral vascular diseases, cancer, diabetes, hypertension, and arthritis prevent us from attaining the goal. And, as I've already discussed, most of these degenerative diseases can be traced to dietary indiscretion.

What Is Gerontology?

Gerontology is a comparatively new field of study. *Dorland's Medical Dictionary* defines it as "the scien-

tific study of the problems of aging in all aspects—
clinical, biological, historical, and sociological."

From the beginning of time, man has been both
perplexed and intrigued by the processes of aging. In
the Far Eastern cultures, especially in China, this
stage of life has been longed for, accepted, and ven-
erated. However, in the United States, aging is both
feared and dreaded.

We cannot deal with every phase of this subject
here, but let us see what some specialists in gerontology have found in their research.

Many gerontologists and other medical scientists
have come to the conclusion that two of the most vital
factors in retarding the aging process are dieting and
exercise. This substantiates my own observations and
clinical experiences.

An interesting and erudite study on this subject was
made by Dr. Alexander Leaf, Chief of Medical Services at Massachusetts General Hospital in Boston,
who journeyed to "several places in the world where
it is not unusual for people to live to the age of one
hundred and still retain their health and vigor. Such
pockets of longevity are to be found in the Andean
area of Ecuador, the Caucasus Mountains of Russia
and in the State of Hunza in Pakistan." Dr. Leaf's article, "Observations of a Peripatetic Gerontologist," in
Nutrition Today, September–October, 1973, continued: "During the past two years, I have visited three
corners of the world where aged individuals are free
of the debilitating diseases that plague our elderly. I
had ample opportunity to observe the dietary customs
and conclude that they would give solace to our nutritionists, who seem to have reached the conclusion
that we must change our eating habits if we are to live
longer. If the United States and Canada had the same
proportion of people who are a hundred or more years
old as one can see in these areas, there'd be nearly
two and a half million centenarians in the two countries. As it is there are only some seven thousand people who have passed the century mark."

He also noted that hard work seems to be another
factor that aids in achieving the goal of longevity. "If

someone told me that James Hilton got his inspiration for his book, *Lost Horizon,* from Hunza, I would believe him. Shangri-la was the home of the ageless who lived in paradise. It was said to be free of tension, which is supposed to play a role in shortening the lives of Western man. The geography of Hunza requires everyone to work hard to eke a living from the sparse terraces. In spite of (or because of) the primitive conditions, one sees an unusual number of vigorous elderly men and women agilely climbing up and down the steep slopes that line the habitable valley of these mountain dwellers."

In his studies Dr. Leaf found that the diets of the Hunza and Vilcabamba people, who live on a very restricted diet, differ from the people in the Caucasus region, who eat everything (but of course not processed foods. He concluded: "According to what we are now being told about the etiology of atherosclerosis, one would say that their low calorie diet, rich in unsaturated fats and vegetables and poor in animal fats, dairy products and sucrose, must account for the longevity of the Hunzakuts and Vilcabambians. But, then, if this is so, what about the Georgians? Their dietary habits and longevity, although different, still give some support to the 'low animal fat, low cholesterol, low caloric' school of thought."

Other prominent gerontologists, after years of meticulous research, have demonstrated a definite correlation between diet and longevity. An article in the San Francisco *Examiner,* by Peter Fraley, stated: "Research into the aging process is demonstrating that the human lifespan can be stretched as much as 30 years. Dr. Leon R. Kass, of the National Academy of Sciences, points out that research into aging and senescence is a field just entering puberty. He cites recent studies that show aging to be a process distinct from disease and one that can be retarded by diet and drugs. A classic study, done in the early 1930's, showed that rats kept on a near-starvation diet lived twice as long as a control group that ate as much as they liked. Recently, Dr. Roy L. Walford of the University of California, Los Angeles, did similar experiments, cutting the diets of rats and mice to a third of the normal caloric intake. He got similar results of increased lifespan and a reduction in the tendency to develop cancer. The exact mechanism for this startling finding remains unknown, but there is indication that it may be due to a strengthening of the body's resistance to disease. However, the reverse is well-known and accepted, that overeating and obesity shorten life in a variety of ways."

Dr. Walford's observations that obesity shortens life in a variety of ways in substantiated by our American society. Insurance company statistics indicate that there are over 50 million overweight Americans. At any given time, men or women, if 20 percent over their ideal weight, have a higher death rate by 20 percent. As the percentage of overweight goes up, the death rate also increases. People who are 30 to 40 percent above normal weight have a 50 percent greater chance of dying than those of normal weight.

The Metropolitan Life Insurance Company stated in its bulletin *Overweight—Its Prevention and Significance*: "Studies were made of a group of men 20% or more overweight and another group of average-weight men with various diseases. The death rate in the overweight group was 40% higher than in the average-weight group in those persons with heart and circulatory disorders. In those with cerebral hemorrhage and other vascular disorders, the death rate was 50% higher in the overweight group than in the average-weight group. In nephritis, 75% higher. The death rate in overweight diabetics was expecially high —more than twice that (133 percent) of the average-weight diabetic."

From this we can only conclude that the way to stop the process of aging and to build up resistance against all diseases is to control our overweight problems.

Dr. Joseph P. Hrachovec, University of Southern California gerontologist, agrees. In his well-documented book on antiaging, *Keeping Younger and Living Longer,* he wrote that it is entirely possible for people to live past the ages of seventy, eighty, and even a hundred years and still be able to enjoy active, healthy lives. People reduce their chances for a longer life, bring on diseases, and make the body wear out too quickly by making three mistakes: (1) by eating improperly, (2) by not exercising, and (3) by not being able to relax.

Dr. Bernard Strehler, University of California professor of biology, stated that ". . . man can find means to increase his lifespan by 15 to 30 years. For example, animal experiments have shown that the effects of dietary restriction alone can increase lifespan—increasing longevity cannot be brought about without increasing the quality of old people's health. With good health, people in the 65 to 85 bracket might well remain employed and not become a burden . . . postponement of physical and mental senescence will mean that a person of 60 would have the outlook of a person of 50; the person of 70, the outlook of a person of 56; and a person of 90, the outlook of a person of 70. There would be new opportunities for self-development that a period of 40 to 50 years of healthy and vigorous life would offer to mothers following child rearing and to fathers for further training and work."

Although all these authorities criticize the American diet, none has specific recipes to correct the dietary indiscretions. I hope this book will help fill that gap.

Effects of the Dong Diet

The following clinical cases show the role the Dong Diet can play in attaining the goal of longevity:

Mrs. R. W. of California was previously mentioned in *The Arthritic's Cookbook*. In 1972 she was Miss R. H., age seventy-three, who hobbled into my office on a cane for consultation. Her knees, hands, and ankles were badly affected with osteoarthritis. Miss R. H. weighed 170 pounds at her first examination, and she was taking 16 aspirins daily. The aspirins were immediately stopped, and she was told to adhere to a stringent diet of fish and vegetables (excluding rice, bread, and potatoes until her weight was re-ing medicine, and only on a part-time basis. If I had not changed my nutritional habits long ago, I am certain that I would have been listed among the deceased in the vital statistics of my class, instead of carrying on a full program of my life's work.

Statistics show that in the United States the high-earning social groups have a higher death rate. Physicians and surgeons in the prime of life lead the parade to the cemetery, followed by lawyers, judges, and business executives—and the lowest death rates are among laborers and farmers. This high death rate among the highly skilled is not only a personal loss to the family and friends but a great loss to our nation.

The science of gerontology has exposed some of the secrets of the process of aging. The outstanding factors are proper diet and exercise. Only a little discipline on anyone's part is required to carry out a longevity program.

Recently, Jack Benny died at the age of eighty. At his tearful funeral service, attended by all the Hollywood greats, Bob Hope said wryly: "He was stingy to the end. He was only with us for eighty years." If any of my readers leave this wonderful world before a hundred years of age, you, too, are being stingy with your experience, knowledge, and skills.

7

Acupuncture: Its Role in My Treatment of Arthritis

In 1971 former-President Nixon's visit to China parted the Bamboo Curtain for the first time in twenty-five years to give us a fascinating glimpse of the sleeping giant. Things of Chinese origin suddenly became intensely interesting to everyone. Books on Chinese history and art enjoyed renewed popularity. Documentaries on China's way of life and activities were on television constantly. Professors, scientists, politicians, and celebrities all wrote about their experiences after visiting mainland China.

Groups of prominent physicians, surgeons, and medical scientists were invited by the Chinese Medical Association to observe firsthand the health-care systems of China and to exchange ideas with their doctors. The majority were astounded at China's medical progress and came back to praise the system. But a few came back to criticize.

The most controversial medical modality has been the use of acupuncture for the treatment of diseases and especially in the field of anesthesia. Because of stories that were circulated about "miracle cures" and the u~   puncture in major operations, the Amer-
                           manded that our conservative medical
                           nvestigate acupuncture and perhaps in-
                           o our medical system. Today, in many
                           chools, research programs on acupunc-
                           ried out.

112

contact with traditional Chinese medicine and acupuncture. Many of my friends and patients told stories of people who had been treated by conventional medical procedures for various chronic ailments without success, and who claimed they had been cured by acupuncture in a short time. Since I had been thoroughly inculcated in scientific medicine, I continued to scoff at such ancient modes of treatment. I theorized, like many of my Western colleagues, that any improvement by acupuncture was a matter of psychology, mesmerism, hypnotism, or the result of a placebo effect.

My third encounter with acupuncture was in 1960. One of my golfing companions is a Far Eastern industrial tycoon. His "secret ambition" in life is to beat me at golf. He regularly spends about two months in the United States trying to accomplish this feat, keeping me constantly supplied with golf balls. During one of his strenuous drives on the golf course, he injured his back and shoulders. An acute condition of this kind could be due to any number of causes, and for diagnosis he was referred to the best specialist in San Francisco. After two months of conventional treatment and physiotherapy, he still could not swing a golf club. In fact, his condition was getting worse. The diagnosis of his problem was osteoarthritis and lumbar intervertebral disk syndrome. Because of his "advanced" age and lack of response to the treatments, the prognosis was a grave one. He was told that he might never be able to play golf again. I had visions of losing not only a golfing pal, but also my source of free golf balls.

Due to the urgency of business, the industrialist had to go back to the Far East. The next summer, when he returned, he was able to swing his clubs better than before. He told me that after he had gone home, he was treated by a master acupuncturist, and in a matter of a few weeks, he was playing golf again. In fact, his game had improved to the point where he could play me on even terms. When his two-month visit was up, he insisted that I go back with him to the Far East to investigate acupuncture more thoroughly.

All the threads of my experiences were beginning to come together, with the result that I began to have a new and less-biased opinion of acupuncture. Reasoning that I did need to get away, my wife and I went to Taipei for a three-week vacation.

Like "The Man Who Came to Dinner," I stayed several months, not only in Taipei but also in Japan and Hong Kong, studying the principles and techniques of acupuncture. I was amazed at the many complicated cases of whiplash, low-back syndrome, "frozen shoulder," various types of arthritis, and other painful conditions that were relieved by acupuncture. My observations of modern methods of treatment had revealed that such cases are usually resistant to therapy.

Techniques of Acupuncture

For those of you who have not seen a demonstration of acupuncture treatments, let me give you a brief description of the technique. The needles are now usually made of stainless steel, are very thin, and come in various lengths, from one to two inches long. They are inserted into the skin and muscles of the patient at specific points, known as meridian points, all over the body. There are 150 to 800 points charted on the front and back of the body, the number varying from one school of acupuncture to another.

For the successful treatment of different diseases, the acupuncturist must learn delicacy of execution, such as the depth and direction of placement of the needles; subtlety of manipulation and stimulation of the meridian points; and proper combinations of meridian points on the body for various diseases.

Recent research has introduced electroacupuncture, which seems to be much more efficient than the older method of manual stimulation of meridian points. The instrument used is a transistorized device powered by a nine-volt battery. Wires from this instrument are attached to various needles that have been inserted into the body.

The Status of Acupuncture in Europe and the United States

On my annual vacations to various parts of the world, I usually try to investigate acupuncture and consult with physicians who are practicing it. Acupuncture was introduced into Europe as early as the seventeenth century, and practically every European country has an acupuncture society made up of doctors of medicine who use this therapy as an adjunctive treatment. About two thousand physicians practice it in France, and the French National Health Service acknowledges acupuncture and pays for the service.

As I mentioned before, acupuncture has literally taken America by storm. However, I predict that unless the medical establishment and the American public are better informed about it, including its limitations, this new therapeutic tool will very soon fall into disrepute and will be discredited and condemned.

All over the country unscrupulous groups are setting up acupuncture clinics and institutes and are hiring so-called Asian acupuncturists, who have not had the proper background in medicine and surgery, to teach them where to insert the needles so they can claim to cure all diseases. These places of deception and delusion are run like assembly lines, and hundreds of patients are seen daily. This cannot possibly be considered proper health-care management, and some states are now beginning to legislate against such facilities.

Hundreds of physicians are also being exploited by "academies of acupuncture," or whatever euphemistic names they use. In various cities throughout the country, these promoters give three-day lectures and workshops in acupuncture, charging exorbitant prices to attend. There is absolutely no way that the techniques of acupuncture can be learned in three days—or even in three months.

This misuse of acupuncture must be stopped, or the yawning cultural gap between China and the West, which has been partially bridged by the Western interest in acupuncture, may be widened.

Medical Training in Mainland China

In mainland China, acupuncture is considered only one method of treatment. Physicians are trained in medical schools similar to those in the United States, with traditional Chinese medicine as a part of their studies.

Let me emphasize that acupuncture is just one of the many disciplines in the curriculum of Chinese medical students, which includes anatomy, histology, neurology, pharmacology, surgery and other standard courses. Acupuncture is not used indiscriminately to treat every disease known to mankind, as some of the "quickie clinics" are doing here in the United States. Many of you have seen television programs of Chinese surgeons performing major surgery such as the removal of brain tumors, lungs, ovarian cysts, and even open-heart surgery and other surgical feats that we perform here in the United States. These surgeons are not treating their cases with acupuncture. They are using acupuncture to stop the pains accompanying surgical operations. This is called an analgesic procedure. What is amazing is that the patients being operated upon are still awake, speaking, and drinking liquids. For most major surgery here, we put the patient to sleep with a general anesthetic.

None of the so-called "master" acupuncturists who are performing here have been trained as physicians in the People's Republic of China. Western medicine was integrated with traditional Chinese medicine only after 1969, and no young medical school graduates have been allowed to leave China for the United States since that time.

They have been trained, if at all, through devious

sources, because even though acupuncture has been used in China for over four thousand years, its popularity and usage depended on the whims and desires of the ruling classes. Since the beginning of this century, changes in the government have also affected the system of medicine. All recent governments have recognized that Western medicine is superior because of its scientific approach. When the Manchu Republic was deposed in 1911 and China became a republic, traditional Chinese medicine was actually prohibited by law. But like the prohibition of liquor in the United States, passing an unpopular law does not mean universal acceptance of or adherence to it. As a matter of fact, only a few officials and the affluent upper class patronized the Western-trained doctors. The masses clung to the traditional methods of treatment.

I want to remind the reader that acupuncture, with all its fascination, mystery, and merits, is but one tool of treatment. Like the use of aspirin, indomethacin, and other drugs, as well as physiotherapy and ultrasound, it does not remove the cause of the disease. In my treatment for arthritis, nutrition is of primary importance; acupuncture and other modes of therapy are ancillary. I believe the following cases will show the effectiveness of this treatment.

NAME:	Mr. G. P.
AGE:	38
OCCUPATION:	Pharmacist
RESIDENCE:	Wyoming
DIAGNOSIS:	Lumbar intervertebral disk syndrome
PREVIOUS MEDICATION:	Aspirin, Darvon, codeine
FIRST VISIT:	November 2, 1973
INTERVIEWED:	November 10, 1973

"I had this back trouble since October, 1968, with pains running down my right thigh. I took some pain medicine which helped me a little. But the condition progressed until it got so bad that I was sent to see some specialists in Salt Lake City.

"They took myelograms and told me that I had lumbar disk disease that was probably due to an old football injury. My pains got worse, so they decided to operate on me. They removed a disk from the lumbar area in 1969. When I recovered from surgery, I felt good for about three months. One day I sat in a chair and I could not get up from it at all; I was in terrible pain. My doctor wanted to operate on me again in a region higher up on the back. But since the first operation didn't help me much, I felt the second operation would not either. I continued to take medicines to help the pain while I worked.

[When Mr. G. P. came in to see me, recommended by another patient, he looked like an old man. He was almost unable to bend over and reported severe pains in his back and legs. I put him on the diet and gave him acupuncture treatments.]

"One week later, I can get out of the chair, sit down and get up again. I can lift my leg, and I can tie my shoes. These are the things that I have not been able to do for three years. It sounds unreal, but it happened. It was very fortunate for me because no one knows what suffering is until they have had the kinds of pains that I have had."

[On Christmas, 1973, Mr. G. P. sent me a note and said, "I am still doing very well. Hell of a diet to get used to. Merry Christmas."]

NAME:	Mr. A. C.
AGE:	51
OCCUPATION:	Produce broker
RESIDENCE:	Idaho
DIAGNOSIS:	Osteoarthritis, cervical and thoracic spine; lumbar intervertebral disk syndrome

PREVIOUS
> MEDICATION: Aspirin, codeine, Darvon,
>   Butazolidin, Percodan, and others
> FIRST VISIT: March 15, 1974
> INTERVIEWED: July 23, 1974

"For about twenty years I have had pains in my neck and back. I have been to many doctors in Idaho. All the doctors told me that there was nothing that they could do about it. I took pain tablets day and night for years. Finally one day I made up my mind to cut them all out. I learned to bear the pains and only took them if the pains were such that I could not stand it any more.

"In 1970 I had an auto accident which flipped me over and crushed my right knee. I began having severe pains in the middle and lower parts of my back that I had never had before. I could not bend my knees at all, and could only bend from my waist. I was examined and treated at the University of Utah, but they too told me that there was nothing that could be done for me. I was then referred to Mayo Clinic. Many x-rays and examinations were done there and the results were the same. Nothing could be done for me.

[On March 15, 1974, I started Mr. A. C.'s treatment by putting him on the diet, and giving him acupuncture treatments. At that time he weighed 205 pounds. He now weighs 184 pounds.]

"After the first three treatments, I did not have any pains in my neck at all. After suffering twenty years with this pain, this was great! My knee and back is not all well yet—but it doesn't hurt nearly like it did. It has been only six weeks since I started treatments.

"Before the auto accident I was active in sports, even though I had the pains. I would play golf and take time off to ski. But since the auto accident in 1970, I was not able to participate in any sports at all.

The other day, though, I played a whole game of golf. Of course, my score was not too good."

NAME: Mr. M. C.
AGE: 27
OCCUPATION: Unemployed
RESIDENCE: California
DIAGNOSIS: Sciatica, left side; osteoarthritis, left hip

PREVIOUS
  MEDICATION: Aspirin, codeine, Darvon, Percodan, Demerol, Dilaudid
FIRST VISIT: April 5, 1973
INTERVIEWED: February 2, 1974

"On April 14, 1967, I was run over by a city bus. I was severely injured. I had a shattered pelvis with a dislocated head of the femur. I had agonizing pains in my left hip from that moment on. I was confined in a hospital for one and half months with a body cast and all kinds of contraptions on me. After my discharge from the hospital, I must have consulted about twenty-five specialists—just trying to get rid of the constant and terrible pains. They started in my left hip, went down to the thigh and then to the leg. The doctors started me off with large doses of aspirin and codeine. I took so much of it that they had to give me antacids to counteract my stomach upset. About a year ago, the pains were so bad that the doctors gave me all kinds of pain pills, Darvon, Percodan, Demerol and finally Dilaudid. I did not want to become an addict, but the pains were so bad that I had to take the medicine.

"My mother heard about Dr. Dong and made an appointment for me.

[Mr. M. C. was a burly young man, six feet tall, with long hair, who limped into my office with the aid of a homemade cane. His attitude indicated frustration, disappointment, and perhaps hostility. He had, no doubt, suffered much pain, agony, and distress.

If he was antiestablishment, he had a right to be. For here was a person who had been treated by many specialists for a period of six years with little result. He was a perfect example of the statement in Medical Opinion: *"He's crippled by pain, 'hooked' on medication, burdened by bills."*

After reading the medical history that he brought to my office, I told Mr. M. C. that there was no way in which I could possibly help him. At his insistence, because he claimed that I was his last hope, I explained my theory of treatment and the dietary regimen. I told him that if he expected to have any results, this program that I was outlining to him would have to be adhered to minutely and religiously.

My previous experiences with this type of case have been unsuccessful for two reasons: first, multiple fractures, especially of the hip, and shortening of the leg, with intractable pains, create abnormal conditions after healing that are very difficult to diagnose and treat. For six years after the accident, Mr. M. C. had been sent by the insurance company from one specialist to another for treatment, without result; and second, in the meantime, the patient had acquired a second disease, addiction to medication (Demerol and Dilaudid), which created another difficult medical problem, not only physical, but also sociopsychological.

He agreed to follow my instructions and I started him on the diet and on acupuncture treatments.]

"I weighed 207 pounds at the beginning of my treatments. Now I weigh 175 pounds. After the first two treatments, I had no pains or problems for three weeks—it was unbelievable. I don't know what happened, but I was able to sleep for eight hours a night and I could walk around flat-footed and move. Remember that my left leg is shorter due to the auto accident, and I could never walk flat-footed. I just had no problems. I had cut down on the pills a lot. Then after three weeks, the pains came back again. I had to take the pills again, but after Dr. Dong gave me another treatment, the pains disappeared like magic again. Each month, when I went in to see him, I improved. Today I have absolutely no pains. I have since moved to Chico, California, where I had taken a job. It is rather cold up there. I have been feeding the wood fire in my house with oak wood that I chop myself. You know how hard oak wood is. I have been working in the almond orchards chopping brush and I have been able to walk reasonable distances, like a mile or two. I have done more hard work in the last month than I have done in the last six years. And I take no pills at all."

In this particular case, the Dong Diet and acupuncture and the cooperation of the patient produced a result that I never expected. This is the type of case that gives me immense joy and satisfaction.

8

Summing Up

Victor Hugo once said, "There is nothing more powerful than an idea whose time has come." In medicine the idea whose time has come is *nutrition's relation to diseases*. Medical scientists are at last beginning to realize that dietary prudence does play an important role in the etiology and treatment of diseases. The American public is beginning to be greatly concerned about nutrition. Patients are beginning to clamor for dietary instructions from their physicians. Consumers are beginning to pay attention to labels, and the government has set up various agencies for the intensive study of food and nutrition in relation to public health.

Throughout this book I have quoted physicians and medical scientists who have definitively demonstrated that many diseases are nutritionally related. Heart disease, strokes, hypertension, diabetes, obesity, and even cancer have been linked to improper diet. I have tried to explain my own profound concern about the relationship between nutrition and rheumatic diseases. I am confident that the medical community, especially those involved in the research and treatment of arthritis, will eventually stop ignoring the probability of the correlation between these two factors.

Nutrition Research Needed

It is important that this country no longer be a nation of nutritional illiterates. It is even more important that physicians and scientists remember that receptivity to new ideas and new avenues of research should be their fundamental consideration. I refer you again to those appalling statistics from government surveys showing that in 1966 there were 17,000,000 arthritics requiring medical care. The fact that this number increased by 1970 to 20,230,000 demonstrates that today's medical techniques of treatment and prevention are abject failures.

These statistics alone should be enough to arouse serious scientific discourse and stimulate research as to whether or not there is validity in the hypothesis that dietary indiscretion may cause arthritis.

Medicine Is Still an Art—Not an Exact Science

In my introductory chapter I told how, as a young physician, I discovered a successful method of treating arthritis, but I was not ready to challenge medical orthodoxy because of my lack of experience. Now after all these years of experience, and with files of thousands of case histories of patients who have been successfully treated with my new therapy, I am still not challenging orthodoxy—or anyone's concepts. Experience in the medical world has given me humility. There are too many intangibles and unanswered questions in the practice of medicine. It is still an art —not an exact science.

My own experience with arthritis not only opened new horizons for me, but it changed my entire perspective of life. I have received great satisfaction from the recovery of my many patients. Writing this book and recalling the various case histories has given me as much genuine pleasure as when these recoveries occurred.

New Philosophy of Life

When I was younger I wanted to shout from the housetops about my new great discovery on nutrition. However, maturity has given me a more philosophical point of view concerning the various aspects of life. I realize that I did not discover food and nutrition. Other physicians in the past have advocated common sense in eating.

When I was afflicted with arthritis, destiny had already prepared me for the position on its treatment that I would eventually take. As a boy, I worked on a farm, havesting crops of vegetables and fruit. I was a professional cook during many of my school vacations. I investigated the preparation of food in slaughter houses and canneries. Thus I was well prepared for putting into practice my new concept of the relationship of food to arthritis.

If my colleagues ignore nutrition in the treatment of their patients, there are extenuating circumstances. Medical school curricula do not include nutrition in their course of study. Our years of pragmatic training were, of course, necessary to learn the fundamentals of the human body and its pathology. But we also acquire a "professorial syndrome" and become conformists. Although conformity is both confining and abrasive, most of us would not think of questioning the concepts of medical orthodoxy in the treatment of diseases—especially arthritis.

If, and when, the subject of nutrition is included in the medical curricula, merely giving lectures and teaching the theory of nutrition will be insufficient. In this respect, medicine is only a descriptive science. The students who become doctors will have much difficulty in translating this theoretical knowledge into practical advice for their patients. The theory of nutrition does not teach them how to cook or prepare a meal.

Teaching Nutrition to Medical Students Is Imperative

One of the most cherished experiences of my life was living at Taliesin West, the home of Frank Lloyd Wright, for two weeks. In 1954, I commissioned Mr. Wright to design a building for me on Telegraph Hill. During that short stay in Arizona, I learned how the architectural genius trained his students.

His students are given a liberal education. Everyone is required to cultivate the land, plant and harvest crops, prepare and cook the food, serve other students, and be served. In the evenings there are different program-lectures in art, philosophy, and literature, and on other occasions classical dancing and concerts are offered.

After the student is thoroughly inculcated in the humanities and in the social and physical sciences, then, and only then, is he taught the fundamentals of architecture. Such an architect cannot help but be a superior one, well educated, cultured, and conscientious.

We need a similar program in medicine to give more practical experience to the student, especially in the fields of diet and nutrition. I wish all medical students were required during their summer vacations to learn agriculture, and to learn all about cooking and food preparation. In this way we could produce physicians who are superior in every phase of life. To paraphrase Dr. Alfred D. Klinger, such doctors would then understand that nutrition is the cornerstone of life. They would know how to apply it properly to sustain the body and the mind. They would be able to teach their patients that the neglect of proper nutrition can cripple them.

In conclusion, I hope that the goals of this book have been accomplished. It was designed for the millions who are suffering from arthritis, but anyone can derive benefit from its information on diet and nutrition and how it is important to change the eating habits of the American people to a more sensible pattern. Remember also that this book and its dietary regimen is an auxiliary treatment for arthritis. You may have other physical conditions besides arthritis that require remedial measures, so you will still need the advice and care of your own physician.

I hope that this book will be of value also to the physicians themselves. More importatnly, however, is the fact that the understanding of the science of nutrition may improve the doctors' own health, so that they may continue to help others.

Mrs. Banks and I have collaborated in translating my hypothesis of treatment into something definitive and comprehensive. In the section that follows, there are menus to make it easier to maintain the diet for longer periods of time, shopping and cooking tips to facilitate daily meal preparation, and many new recipes which will show you the wide variety of dishes you can prepare from the foods that are allowed on the Dong Diet.

THE MECHANICS

9

It's What You Don't Eat That Counts

Before going into the how-to—the implementation—of the diet, let's clear up any misunderstanding of the basic principles. Some may think that simply consuming masses of fish and vegetables is going to do the trick—never mind the dab of hollandaise on the broccoli, never mind the little glass of orange juice without which it is impossible to start the day!

Let me say here and now, as firmly as possible: It isn't what you eat that does it as much as what you do *not* eat! Success depends on a strict adherence to the following lists, to the avoidance of the foods and additives designated as no-noes. The smallest infractions *do* make a difference. Dr. Dong's diet is essentially an extremely simple one, and there's no reason in the world why it can't be a pleasant and satisfying one. Herewith your list of do's and don't's:

DO EAT:

All seafood
All vegetables, including avocados
Vegetable oils, particularly safflower oil
Margarine (if possible, free of milk solids)
Egg whites
Honey
Nuts, sunflower seeds, soybean products
Rice of all kinds (brown, white, or wild)
Bread to which nothing on the "Don't" list has
    been added
Tea and coffee
Plain soda water
Parsley, onions, garlic, bay leaf, salt
Flour (preferably the more nutritious unbleached
    and whole-grain)
Sugar (as little as your sweet tooth demands)
Chicken broth

PERHAPS OCCASIONALLY:

Breast of chicken
A *small* amount of wine in cooking
A *small* drink of bourbon or vodka
A *small* pinch of spicy seasoning such as curry
    powder
Noodles or spaghetti (since the amount of egg
    is relatively small and somewhat broken down
    in the cooking)

DO NOT EAT:

Meat in any form, including broth
Fruit of any kind, including tomatoes
Dairy products, including egg yolks, milk, cheese,
    and yogurt

Vinegar, or any other acid

Pepper (most definitely) of any variety

Hot spices

Chocolate

Dry roasted nuts

Alcoholic beverages, particularly wine

Soft drinks (I've never found one without additives)

All additives, preservatives, chemicals, most especially monosodium glutamate. (One exception to this rule is lecithin in margarine.)

EXCEPTIONS:

In addition to the very occasional exceptions allowed above, there are other unavoidable exceptions. Sensitivity to certain foods will vary from person to person; this must be determined by the individual. Allergies to certain seafoods, for instance, or accompanying diseases such as gout or colitis, will require a personalized selection. In gout, or gouty arthritis, vegetables such as asparagus, spinach, artichokes, peas, beans, and mushrooms are possible offenders; in some colitis cases it might be necessary to cook all vegetables. In other words, take a commonsense approach to what is essentially a commonsense diet! For those allergic to shellfish, I suggest a menu of fish and the later addition of chicken or turkey breast. For those allergic to *all* seafood, I can only suggest the white meat of chicken or turkey. These unfortunates must settle for deriving what benefit they can from a restricted regime. Again, it's not what you *do* eat that counts, it's what you *don't!*

At the outset, the diet may seem formidable, I admit, for in the beginning even chicken breasts must be eliminated by those seriously affected by arthritis until there has been a definite improvement in their condition. *The Arthritic's Cookbook* was written to introduce this diet to arthritis sufferers and to demonstrate how one could follow it and still have varied, tasty, and even gourmet meals. In answer to many requests, in the pages that follow I am going to go into much more detail on various aspects of implementing the diet as well as share with you many additional recipes I think are easy, economical, and make marvelously satisfying dishes. For those new to the diet, I'm also going to give suggested menus to take you through the first week, followed by a plan to complete a month. Use your good common sense and experiment to determine what suits you best. Remember, we are all a little different, one from the other. Don't fight your individual tastes! The range of foods is wide enough to include *something* you like, I feel sure! There's no reason to force yourself to eat things you dislike. I'm not mad for beets, for instance. Alfalfa sprouts, on the other hand, are a great favorite; they're a good food, economical, and easy to grow in the kitchen window. (If you'd rather buy them, many supermarkets now carry them.)

The suggested foods make up a sensible diet containing protein, vitamins, minerals, and carbohydrates in digestible, acceptable form. The reduction in calories alone will be of immeasurable benefit; the fact that the body is being given only what it needs cannot help but improve the general health.

Obviously, however, not everyone will be able to adhere to such a strict regime all the time, day in and day out. Some office workers can "brown-bag" it, for instance; others cannot. If a restaurant has no fish, try to get a sandwich made of white meat of chicken, and failing that, try for tuna or peanut butter; it's almost always possible to get raw carrots or celery to accompany the sandwich. Salads are a good compromise; a tuna salad with a little mayonnaise, even if it's not safflower-oil mayonnaise, is certainly going to be preferable to a hamburger! You might settle for a vegetable plate, as you can always make up the protein at the next meal. Incidentally, remember that the white of the hard-boiled egg is protein!

Experience will teach you what is most harmful to you when you find you *must* deviate. I don't eat anything but the salad and French bread on the airlines, as they use additives to preserve the flavor of the rewarmed food. (You can always have a nice little sandwich tucked away in your carry-on bag, however.) On the other hand, I often find it very hard to explain to a hostess who's gone to no end of trouble that I "don't eat meat" or "can't have chocolate mousse." But which is more important, an embarrassed apology or your lifelong health?

Longevity is the eternal dream, of course. We all know we'll die someday; on the other hand, I'm sure there are very few among us who don't like to feel we are doing all in our power to maintain a long and healthy life span. We *can* furnish our bodies with just the fuel necessary—no more, no less.

Above all, we must not gain weight. Think of a one-ton automobile and imagine that after ten years' use a ton and a half is its burden. Would you take this car out of the garage, expecting it to stand up under this added strain? Our nutrition should be looked upon in the same way; we should, as we age, consume foods that do not overload the body. Is it not preferable, perhaps essential, to allow the poor machine to function unhampered?

The analogy between an automobile and our bodies is quite appropriate; many of the additives and detergents we are urged to run through our automobile engines seem to result in a repair bill. We should also remember that exercise is vital to the life process; exercise stimulates the circulation, helps throw off poisons through breathing and perspiration. Just like an automobile, the body that's functioning well due to proper care will not deteriorate so fast—in other words, will live longer.

According to Dr. Alex Comfort, experiments with animals have shown the way to expand human life spans by twenty to forty years and to lessen the chances of heart disease and cancer. "Longer life span is probably available now—for the young, if not the successful middle-aged, though they would gain," he says. The British scientist feels the way to do it is by simply limiting the calorie intake to 60 percent of what we now eat (a reduction of one-third). Or, he suggests, full-feeding for two days and fasting for one would accomplish the same thing. "The foods to cut

down are starch, sugar, dairy produc
Comfort points out. "This applies to c
as adults." It is interesting to note that t
very same items that are either eliminateo
pedaled in Dr. Dong's diet for arthritics.

When you change to the diet, there's no need to el
that you must change your entire way of life! Growth
and fulfillment need not stop just because of arthritis!
Nor must the pleasures of life be set aside. Go out, get
involved, broaden your horizons all around. Above
all, live! Your arthritis will benefit, your world will
look brighter, and you'll look brighter to all those
around you.

10

Planning and Buying

After considerable inquiry and research, I've discovered that it's quite possible to follow Dr. Dong's regime anyplace in the United States. Easier, granted, where fresh fish and vegetables abound, but certainly not impossible in other places. This is a broad, rich, and varied land!

My food bills are most certainly below those of my meat-, fruit-, and dairy-product-consuming friends. There's no doubt that in these days of soaring prices the food dollar will stretch farther when expended for the less expensive fish—fresh *or* frozen—and vegetables—such as carrots, onions, potatoes, green beans, and spinach. And the price of sugar hardly concerns us, as there is practically no use for it in this diet. Once you start using all your leftovers in soups, saving old bread for crumbs, even making your own bread if possible, I think you'll find you're way ahead financially as well as nutritionally.

The crowded, well-stocked refrigerator is no longer to be desired. The fresher your foods and the quicker they get to your table, the fewer chemicals you're likely to consume. And at today's prices, who can afford to throw away any spoiled food? On the other hand, it's good economics to plan, buy, and cook ahead. If you have a busy week ahead or know you will be late getting home some night, it's a comforting feeling to know there's a tuna or oyster casserole in the freezer waiting to be popped in the oven.

Allot a free morning to plan and cook ahead. Plot out your menus, assemble all your ingredients, and cook everything more or less at once. Your bread or English muffins can be rising while you peel the vegetables. You'll have to concentrate on watching a lot of things at once, and you'll feel somewhat like the chef of a famous restaurant overseeing his domain. Make your Chicken Broth, your Court Bouillon, and your Fish Stock (see the recipe section, pages 169–170), and store them either in the refrigerator or in the freezer, according to when you plan to use them. (They all freeze nicely.)

When buying vegetables, try to keep in mind you should have some of the root vegetables, some of the leafy green, some raw, and some cooked every day. It's usually possible, anywhere and at any time of year, to buy fresh carrots, celery, onions, and potatoes. These can be kept on hand or cooked for use later, along with such vegetables as beets, green beans, brussels sprouts, and zucchini. It's handy to have a ready supply of cold vegetables, slightly undercooked, to serve cold with an oil dressing either as a lunch dish or as a salad at dinner. I buy parsley in a sizable amount, chop it, and keep it in a jar in the refrigerator. Parsley is rich in vitamins and minerals. It is also easy to grow either outdoors or in a pot in the kitchen window.

I prefer to steam vegetables in order to save as many of the minerals and vitamins as possible. The water left in the bottom of the steamer is always saved for soup, as are all leftover vegetables including celery and beet tops. Incidentally, cooking vegetables destroys the enzymes, those valuable triggers; this is why raw vegetables are especially valuable, and you will want to make use of both kinds.

Don't neglect the basic canned items like tuna, chopped clams, and oysters when making your casseroles. These items are less expensive to start with, and lots of tasty dishes can result. I think I've made a Tuna Casserole (see pages 196 and 197) almost every Monday night for years, and so far, no complaints.

Clam spaghetti with canned chopped clams is a family favorite for Sunday nights.

This way of preparing food is really somewhat a return to the old basics and a simpler way of life, certainly more in keeping with the times than packaged foods and frozen dinners! But on top of that, when well prepared, this food has a simple elegance that's hard to beat!

The purchasing of these foods is of the utmost importance, of course. But before doing any buying, make a complete and careful check of all the labels already on your shelves for anything with additives or preservatives in it, and get rid of these items.

Although the Food and Drug Administration continually investigates the thousands of additives being used in food processing today, it is practically impossible to demonstrate absolute proof of safety of an additive for everyone. And try as it may, the FDA simply cannot begin to control food manufacturing in this country; the majority of food and drug inspectors are overworked, grossly underpaid public servants. The FDA estimates that food poisoning has increased in the United States more than 1,000 percent since 1951. National Health Surveys report that digestive disturbances affect an estimated eight million people a year. To these figures, add the uncounted illnesses, allergies, and health damage caused by additives, and you have a truly frightening picture.

We should be highly suspicious of any synthetic chemical that accumulates in the body. Although we don't yet know which chemicals cause or affect arthritis, we do know it is a biochemical disturbance more than one of wear and tear. For this reason additional chemicals can only make the disease worse; what the well person may be resistant to can be extremely harmful to the sick person. In a previous chapter Dr. Dong has listed some of the more commonly used additives, and it follows that we want to ingest as little of these as possible.

Geneticist James A. Crow wrote in "A Lethal Legacy," *Science Year*, 1971:

It would be revealing to take a closer look at the incredible number of other man-made chemicals now found in our air, food, water, and even our medicine cabinets. Some of these, such as drugs and food additives, we consume on purpose. Others like sulfur dioxide and nitrates, we take in helplessly in our polluted air and water. But we know little of how any of these chemicals affect us, because persons living today are the first to have ever been exposed to many of them. These chemicals threaten us in four ways: they can poison us, cause cancer, deform our unborn children in the womb, and damage our hereditary material. . . .

In the past, we have been quite reckless in our ignorance. New chemicals have been widely used long before much was known about their long-term effects on either man or wildlife. In my view, many should have learned an important lesson from the cyclamate episode. Never again should we add a substance to the diet of an entire nation without first performing exhaustive tests to determine its potential for both short- and long-term harm to human beings.

Have we paid adequate attention to any of these warnings? How can the arthritic know just how much of his suffering has been chemically induced?

Colman McCarthy, in an article entitled "Bon Chemical Appetit" in *The New Republic*, November 30, 1974, says:

Increased warnings are being sounded about the health dangers of many American foods. It's no longer just the carrot juice and yogurt groupies who worry, but others also, from school nutritionists who don't want their children exposed to government approved and ITT-made Astrofood, to the nation's 104,000 dentists who must yank and fill the teeth rotted by "fun foods." It is not that science and chemicals are dirty words—such a dismissal ignores the many benefits to come from the labs—but that citizens have become an experimental control group.

Just when the public was beginning to realize that a lot of our food products were nutritionally worthless, the manufacturers started "fortifying" them. The worthless food that already had artificial color and flavor added now has vitamins to persuade the consumer to buy. These vitamins, of course, do nothing to counteract the potential damage of the high levels of sugar, fat and salt. Dr. Michael Jacobson, an MIT Ph.D. in microbiology, is with the Center for Science in the Public Interest in Washington. Each year he appears at the annual meeting of food technologists to award his Bon Vivant Vichyssoise Memorial Prize, a garbage can. In 1973 the winner was General Mills for Kaboom, Sir Gracefellow, Baron von Redberry and Franken Berry, all cereals containing 30 and 50 percent sugar. The 1974 award went to Gerber's baby food. *The Wall Street Journal* of January 13, 1975, relates that the H. J. Heinz Co. is recalling about 600,000 boxes of instant dry baby cereal as a result of a *fourth* consumer complaint over metal particles found in the food.

We've gone into detail on these additives and preservatives to help you ascertain which foodstuffs are safe to buy and which aren't. You need to know which are more harmful than others. If you familiarize yourself with their names and initials, and then test your knowledge on the contents of your larder, you'll have an easier time at the market. Your first few shopping trips are apt to be time-consuming, but you'll soon know what items to stay away from and what brands you can safely buy. Don't forget to take your glasses to the store! You must be able to see *everything* that's printed on the label!

Let's start with the basic items that one keeps on hand, such as bread, oil, margarine, and mayonnaise. Shopping for these things is easier today because, thanks to the increased interest in natural foods that began a few years ago, most major cities have health-food stores and many markets have sections devoted to such foods.

Starting with the good old staff of life, you'll want to look for breads whose ingredients list no dairy product or harmful preservative. Some well-known brand names advertise on the package: "no preservatives added," but unfortunately the bread is made with dairy products. Unpolluted breads and muffins are carried in health-food stores; San Francisco French bread, a pure flour and water product, is shipped frozen to many parts of the country. In many places, however, preservatives are forced upon us for economic reasons. The larger chain stores are likely to fill their shelves with the popular, heavily advertised, preserved breads. Many of the smaller towns don't have health-food stores and specialty shops. *But*—and this is important—if the demand is great enough, the product will become available! If you and all your friends start bombarding the stores with requests for healthful breads, eventually you'll get them!

In the meantime, for those in the areas where it's absolutely impossible to procure "real" bread, I strongly suggest making it yourself. It really isn't all that complicated; it's mainly a matter of being around for the rising and kneading processes. In addition, and certainly to be considered in these times, you can make *at least* three loaves for the price of one store-bought loaf. French bread, or a reasonable facsimile thereof, is very easy to make. I bake Whole-Wheat Bread (page 174) and Bran English Muffins (page 173) about every two weeks and freeze what I'm not using in the first week.

After bread, the next staple items you'll want to look for are the oils and margarines. The use of oil is to be preferred over margarine. This does not mean margarine should be eliminated; it is simply used in moderation. The reason is that we try to stay with the foods that are highest in the polyunsaturates, a type of fat effective in reducing the cholesterol level in the blood. The hydrogenization process that the oils must go through in the preparation of the margarine product considerably reduces the polyunsaturates. So try to condition yourself to use oil as much as possible, in cooking and on your vegetables at serving time instead of margarine.

Safflower oil is highest in polyunsaturates and therefore preferable. Sunflower, soybean, corn, cottonseed, sesame, and peanut oils come next. Corn oil is probably the most available and certainly quite acceptable if safflower oil cannot be found. On the other hand, coconut oil, though used in many products and designated a vegetable oil, is actually more highly saturated than butterfat or lard. Unfortunately, safflower oil is hard to find in some sections of the country. If your grocer doesn't have it, your pharmacy may. And it is carried in all health-food stores. Some of the brand names are Hain's, Hollywood, and Norganic. Like most other products, it will be much more expensive in pharmacies and health-food stores than in the markets. Also, beware: Oxidants such as BHT, BHA, or propyl gallate may have been added to some brands, so read those labels carefully before buying.

Safflower margarine will also be highest in the polyunsaturates, and therefore preferable. Again, you may not be able to find it and will have to settle for one of the corn oil margarines or a product called Willow Run made from soybeans. Hain's makes a 100-percent safflower shortening available in health-food stores. (All the Hain's products are good.) You *are* likely to have trouble finding margarine without milk solids, but don't worry because the amount used is rather negligible and not too important. It's much more important to remember to be moderate in the use of margarine. Combine it with oil whenever possible —when using it for browning in cooking, for instance.

Mayonnaise is a very useful adjunct to the diet. I find it useful in cooking as well as a necessity for salads. Dr. Dong allows safflower-oil mayonnaise in spite of the fact that egg is usually listed in the ingredients. Here again, the amount is so negligible it may be ignored. Unfortunately, Saffola Mayonnaise, a very good product, is available only on the West Coast, but Balanaise is its counterpart in the East. And Hain's can be found in most health-food stores.

Peanut butter is a basic of the diet for me; but of course, this is a matter of individual taste. My favorite brand is Laura Scudder's Old Fashioned Style Peanut Butter; it is in its natural state without having been hydrogenated.

Next on the list of staples are the canned seafood items such as tuna. These will probably take up a good bit of space on your kitchen shelves. Geisha tuna is the most purely packed; StarKist is available in most parts of the country. Be sure, however, to buy the solid-pack tuna that says "albacore" on the can. This is a different fish from the regular tuna, smaller and thus less retentive of pollutants such as mercury. I particularly like the StarKist packed in spring water; this is just nice white chunks of tuna without the oily flavor and much nicer for salads and sandwiches. If you can't find tuna packed in water, you can wash out most of the oil by pouring boiling water over it in a sieve.

Snow's minced clams are packed in their natural juices with only salt added. Some brands, unfortunately, Monarch among them, have added MSG to their clams. I buy a brand of small oysters, perfect for soups and chowders, with the Orleans label. These brands are available in the chain stores in most parts of the country. You can find canned shrimp and crab without additives, too, but at a price. When I really feel like splurging I buy a can of shad roe. Browned in a little oil and margarine and served with a baked potato and salad, this makes my all-time favorite dinner.

You will need a supply of clam juice, and here again, you must read the label. I've found the bottled preferable to the canned for lack of additives. Chicken broth, an absolute essential for a good deal of my cooking, is almost impossible to get without MSG; I have never found a canned soup yet that didn't have additives. You will have to make your own, and I'll go more into your homemade supplies later.

Incidentally, it's worth remembering to check your supermarket for specials; there's always the chance of a good buy, particularly in some of the more expensive items.

When it comes to buying vegetables you'll of course want to buy the fresh produce available in season. I'm sure we're all aware by now of the importance of washing fresh produce well to remove any chemicals used to control pests, fertilize, etc. If you must depend almost entirely on frozen vegetables as you may in certain parts of the country, it's no problem because all areas now have good standard brands of frozen vegetables. Read the labels and eliminate all those that have anything added. Unfortunately, most "convenience foods" are out. All those seductive ads on television that tell you how healthful this or that product is will have a list of chemicals on the label long enough to, perhaps, kill a horse! In certain instances, I use a frozen vegetable even though I could use the fresh. I keep a supply of frozen chopped spinach on hand, for instance, for use in many recipes. It's so convenient I forget how much better it would be if I used the fresh. The tiny frozen green peas are great in salad; I just put them in a sieve, pour boiling water over them, and that's all the cooking they need.

We come now to buying fish and chicken. The latter is easy—chicken is available just about everywhere, fresh or frozen. Fresh is best, of course, but frozen will certainly do. If you can, try to buy chicken that hasn't been fed hormones or other undesirable things. On the West Coast Foster Farms is a good brand that advertises its nonuse of hormones (a suspected carcinogen with other cloudy side effects). You'll have to ask about the inclusion of hormones, however, as the law does not as yet require their listing on labels.

Fish is the backbone of this diet. It's our main source of quality protein, so if you don't like fish, just remember that fish likes you. Let me enumerate some of its nutritional properties: Fish has a low-calorie, high-protein content; fishery products are the only sources of animal protein food in which the polyunsaturated fats are found in abundance; the protein of fish contains all of the biologically essential amino acids and is easily broken down by the digestive processes and readily available to the body. Fish contains many dietetically valuable minerals such as iron, phosphorus, calcium, iodine, cobalt, copper, magnesium, potassium, and other trace minerals necessary for the proper operation of the body. Fish is low in sodium content. Fish is rich in vitamins, particularly the B-complex series, which includes niacin, pantothenic acid, B12, riboflavin, thiamine, and pyridoxine. Convinced?

Obviously, if you have a fish market near you, you'll be patronizing it, and equally obviously, with fresh fish available it will be easier to follow the regime. Ask the man in the market to guide you in the selection and kinds and cuts of fish. Truly fresh fish is firm to the touch, has shiny scales and bright eyes; it should smell strongly of the sea, never strongly fishy. Your choice will depend on whether you want to bake a whole fish, to broil fish steaks, to sauté or poach fillets. The main difference in kinds of fish is their fat content; salmon, shad, trout, and mackerel are higher in fat content than sole, halibut, haddock, and perch. All shellfish are considered lean.

Availability and price are seasonal, of course. The producing areas of saltwater fish are the Atlantic, the Pacific, the Gulf of Mexico, and Alaska. The waters off the Atlantic coast produce, in season, bluefish, butterfish, cod, croaker, drum, sea bass, haddock, halibut, herring, mackerel, whiting, mullet, salmon, porgy, sea bass, sea trout, shad, swordfish, ocean catfish, and flounder. The flounder family probably supplies us with a large proportion of our saltwater fish, as on the East Coast it includes blackback, fluke, dab, gray sole, lemon sole, and yellowtail; in southern waters it's called simply flounder, and on the West Coast it encompasses our entire sole family—Dover, English, petrale, and rex. In addition, fish on the Pacific coast include cod, halibut, herring, lingcod, mackerel, rockfish, sablefish, salmon, sea bass, shad, skate, swordfish and tuna. The southern waters of the Gulf produce bluefish, red and black drum, mackerel, whiting, mullet, pompano, sea trout, sheepshead, and red snapper in addition to the aforementioned flounder.

The vast reaches between these coastal areas must depend for their fresh fish on freshwater fish. The Great Lakes has a rich variety: carp, catfish, chub, lake herring and trout, pickerel, sand pike, freshwater drum, smelt, whitefish, lake perch, and wall-eyed pike.

Other lakes will produce some of these, such as carp, catfish, drum, perch, and pike, and the inland rivers supply a large sector of the population with buffalo-fish, carp, catfish, pickerel, drum or sheepshead, trout, and yellow perch.

Catfish is undoubtedly the fresh fish most available the year around. One may be put off a bit by its appearance, but its large head and whiskers are more than offset by the fact that it's inexpensive, and when properly prepared, delicious. I've had catfish from the Missouri River, small ones eight or nine inches long, that have been cooked whole and have the most delicate flaky white meat. Some reasonably priced and reasonably available saltwater fish are flounder, ocean perch, lingcod, scrod, haddock, and butterfish. Sole has risen so in price, it is no longer an inexpensive item, but its virtue for me is that it's almost always available on the West Coast and is easy to prepare in so many tasty ways. Then there are the luxury seasonal items like crab and other shellfish, salmon, and (I can hardly bring myself to mention it) lobster. Still, I suppose if you were eating meat, you'd occasionally blow yourself to a steak.

Unfortunately, only the lucky few are going to have an accessible fish market. However, many supermarkets and grocery stores have fish departments now, though in some cases you're getting fish that was frozen to be shipped, then defrosted slowly in the market's refrigerators. Sometimes you can barely tell the difference, but in any case certain rules as to the handling and storing of frozen fish do prevail. Once thawed, fish must be used immediately, and should not be refrozen. Maximum storage life can be obtained by maintaining the temperature at zero degrees (Fahrenheit) or below and by providing adequate moisture-vapor wrapping or glazing. If fish are placed directly in refrigerated space without protective treatment, a gradual loss of moisture will occur until the fish are shrunken and dried. Dehydration not only causes an unsightly appearance and alteration in texture but also results in loss of weight and flavor.

Many of you will be depending entirely on packaged frozen fish. You must find the brands that have been packaged with no additives and avoid all that have been precooked, breaded, or treated in any way. One good brand, Booth's, is available in many parts of the country. Another I recommend is High Liner. Among the packaged frozen fish are perch, sole, turbot, whiting, trout, and haddock, as well as shellfish such as lobster, carab, and shrimp.

The best method of thawing fish is in your refrigerator, and as noted, it must be used immediately when thawed. The quickest way to thaw, but less desirable than the refrigerator method, is under cold running water, and the least desirable way is thawing at room temperature. This is because the thinner parts of the fish, such as the section near the tail, will thaw faster than other parts and may spoil if the thawing period is long.

Both fresh and frozen fish are sold in various forms, the cut more or less depending on the original size. Small fish are usually sold whole or drawn; medium fish whole or pan-dressed (entrails, head, tail, and fins removed); and larger fish are sold filleted or as steaks. The advantage of the fillet, of course, is that there are practically no bones. Frozen fish are usually filleted.

Servings of fresh and frozen fish generally are based on portions of one-third to one-half pound for each person. Of course when estimating amounts you must take into account the edible portions of whatever form you're considering.

11

And the Cooking...

Fish cookery, both fresh and frozen, has some very definite maxims. Fish must always be cooked gently. Low heat is best, and overcooking is absolutely fatal to the delicate flavor and texture. You really must attend to business when you're cooking fish; you must be on hand to end the cooking at the very instant of completion. Another good rule to remember is that fish cooking is *moist* cooking. You are always cooking it either in a broth such as a Court Bouillon (page 170), baking it covered to retain the juices, basting it, or sautéeing it very quickly.

So, fish can be broiled, poached, sautéed, or baked. Small fish such as trout are best dredged in flour and fried in safflower oil. Mackerel, perch, salmon, sole, turbot, and the like can be poached whole or filleted, a method I find highly satisfactory. I think very few things can equal a piece of poached turbot with a pat of margarine melting on it.

A good, simple way of cooking frozen fish is the poaching method. Cooked haddock can, after poaching, be cut into pieces and made into a casserole. Cover with a cream sauce made by sautéeing chopped onions in oil, working in a little flour and margarine, cooking slightly, and then thinning with a bit of the poaching water. Bake with some bread crumbs sprinkled on top and perhaps seasoned with an herb such as tarragon or basil. This dish can be a very good, inexpensive standby.

Another easily prepared fish is catfish. It has no scales, and the skin will slide off very much like that of the eel. And it can be prepared in chunks because the meat falls away from the bones very easily. However, you may prefer it in steaks or fillets. Either way, dry the pieces well, dip them in egg white slightly beaten with a little water, and cornstarch or flour, then fry them in your oil-and-margarine mixture. You can add chopped parsley to the browned oil to pour over the fish, or you might like a mixture of chopped fresh herbs. For a whole fish, try Catfish with Herbs (page 190) or Catfish Martigues (page 190).

Steaks of any of the larger fish such as haddock can be broiled, and all the larger fish can also be baked in a variety of ways. The shellfish are all delicate and should be handled accordingly. They can be either simmered a few minutes or sautéed just till they turn color.

Don't destroy the marvelous flavor and texture of fish with a lot of herbs and seasonings; just the lightest touch is needed, only enough to bring out the natural flavors. Incidentally, one need hardly salt fish at all, for fish as well as vegetables are rich in natural salts. Fish lends itself to good cooking better than anything else I can think of, and perhaps this is why the French make so much use of their *fruits de mer!*

Obviously, frozen fish is never going to be as good as fresh when simply grilled or broiled, but I've found that frozen sole, halibut, haddock, and trout are all good when handled properly to disguise the change in texture. Frozen fish is apt to be dry due to the loss of moisture, and so must be prepared in a way that will replace that moisture.

The main point to remember is to defrost the fish slowly and thoroughly. Remove it from the package, place it on a plate, and let it defrost slowly in the refrigerator. When it's completely unfrozen and you can separate the pieces without breaking them, lay the fish on paper towels and pat it thoroughly dry. It's then ready to prepare in much the same way as you would with fresh. As I said, I have good luck poaching it, particularly sole, and serving it either with a sauce or flaking it into a casserole with a cream sauce. Amandine—sautéeing it in browning oil and margarine with almonds—is another good way.

Fish cookery is a Mediterranean specialty, particularly in Provence, France, and some of their methods for handling their dryish fish lend themselves nicely to preparing frozen fish. For instance, in Provence a whole fish is placed in a dish, covered with their marvelous olive oil, and allowed to stand in the sun for several hours. It's then removed from the oil and broiled. Halibut steaks and the other large varieties of frozen fish can be improved by an oil marinade. I season my safflower oil with a little good olive oil, perhaps adding an herb or two such as fennel or thyme, and let the defrosted fish rest in it for an hour or so—not necessarily in the sun, however! I also find an hour or so—not necessarily in the sun, however! I also find that just brushing the oil on the fillets before broiling helps counteract the dryness, too.

As a general rule, you can cook frozen fish in any of the ways you'd prepare it fresh, but some methods are just better for preserving the flavor and texture. There are many recipes in *The Arthritic's Cookbook* for cooking frozen sole that could be adapted to other frozen fish fillets. But do be careful to thaw your frozen fish carefully, dry it as suggested, and above all, be extra careful not to overcook!

At the risk of sounding like a nut on the subject of overcooking, I'm going to extend the maxim to frozen vegetables as well. I prefer all vegetables slightly undercooked, both to preserve their wonderful flavor and texture and to preserve as many vitamins and minerals as possible. Potatoes, of course, are an exception. Is there anything worse than an underdone baked potato?

If only a single member of the family is on Dr. Dong's diet, that naturally presents difficulties for the cook. We all know what a nuisance it is to prepare a special meal for one person. The cook gets tired of it, and someone usually gets short shrift. But isn't it possible to explain to the other members of the family the enormous benefits to be derived from this healthy, balanced diet? The man in the family especially will profit. If you have any doubts, consult *The Heart Association Cookbook*. A woman I know, an arthritic, decided to simply start cooking this way for herself and her husband without mentioning it. After he'd been thriving on it for some time, he told her he'd heard about "this fish-and-vegetable diet for arthritis" and suggested she try it. "My dear," she said, "I've been on it for three months, and so have you!" After he'd recovered from his surprise, he realized he felt better than he'd felt in years, his weight was down, and he'd *enjoyed* it!

However, if such cooperation is impossible, it is not difficult for the arthritis sufferer to have his portion of fish or chicken cooked his way, to have the vegetables that would be served in any case, and to skip any dairy products and fruits. But do try to protect the rest of the family from harmful additives and preservatives. We just don't know enough about the evils of these modern poisons. Who knows what unknown troubles you may be saving them from in later life? And to provide a good balance of protein, minerals, and carbohydrates, soft-pedaling the unnecessary, fattening items. Let raw carrots and celery with peanut butter gradually replace the Danish pastry and apple pie à la mode!

12

But What Do You Eat for Breakfast?

Breakfast means tea and toast to me, but I realize that for many it's the most important meal of the day. Some may need protein to support a physically active day; some may require a bit of sugar (I feel I do, so I have a bit of honey on my toast). It's quite possible to satisfy all tastes!

However, the first habit to break—a lifelong habit for most of us—is that glass of orange juice. *Forget* about fruit and fruit juices; simply put them out of your mind. Try substituting a glass of carrot juice. It is a fine source of vitamins and easy to make in a blender. If you feel the day isn't off to a proper start without cereal, by all means have it, but you'll have to get used to eating it without milk or cream. Believe it or not, a little chicken broth isn't bad over cereal, or for cooked cereal, try a little melted margarine.

Here again I must warn you to read the labels. Only a few of the dry cereals are free of additives. Post Grape Nuts, Granola, Heartland, and Quaker 100% Natural Cereal all are, but unfortunately the last-named has nonfat dry milk and cholesterol-high coconut, and Granola has a very high sugar content. Many cereals contain BHT, among them Wheaties, Kellogg's Corn Flakes and Rice Krispies, Nabisco's Team, and Shredded Wheat. General Mills Buc-Wheats has calcium carbonate, artificial flavoring, and BHT, and Kellogg's Concentrate, both BHA and

BHT. The cooked cereals fare better; Wheatena has no additives, nor has Quaker Oats, Roman Meal, or Cream of Rice, but Cream of Wheat has tricalcium phosphate and disodium phosphate. Incidentally, the ratio of carbohydrates to protein is high in all the cereals and should be borne in mind when weight is a factor.

For those of you accustomed to starting the day with an egg, a delicious Egg-White Omelet (page 173) should satisfy. Try it different ways till you find a variation that suits you—with chopped parsley, with a combination of herbs and chives, with thinly sliced celery or green pepper, or even with nuts. My favorite is a combination of thinly sliced green onions and slivers of green pepper. Add a slice or two of French or whole-wheat bread toast, and you have a good, protein-rich breakfast. For those who feel the need for even more protein there's always the English-style breakfast: kippers, finnan haddie, or perhaps a piece of chicken or creamed tuna on toast.

English muffins are good for breakfast; homemade Bran English Muffins are delicious, particularly with honey. Do a little experimenting. For instance, I found I could make perfectly good corn bread by substituting water for milk in the recipe, and simply omitting the egg yolk. Or try steaming some tortillas some morning! Or treat yourself on Sunday morning to French Toast and real maple syrup. Simply soak whole-wheat bread in egg white, slightly beaten with a little water, until the bread soaks up the liquid. Spray a pan with nonstick coating and brown the bread crisply, melt a small pat of margarine on top, add the syrup, and enjoy with lots of good coffee. Who can complain of this as an accompaniment to the Sunday paper?

13

Now We Start

By now you should be all primed with positive thinking and determination. Following this regimen is likely to mean a complete shift in life-style for most people. I have made up a thirty-day menu for those who want definite guidelines. If you meticulously follow this day after day for three meals a day, I don't think you'll have *time* to have arthritis, let alone anything else! You'll be too busy shopping for the ingredients and cooking. However, with some adjustments for leftovers, for availability, and for personal taste, you should then be able to follow the diet on your own. Remember, the white meat of chicken is allowed no more than once a week. And if you are an extreme sufferer, substitute fish for the breast of chicken for about a year. And remember, no deviations whatsoever at any time!

It's probably safe to assume that the great majority of people starting out on the diet are somewhat overweight and could stand to lose about ten pounds. With the elimination of carbohydrates, this can be done in the first two weeks. Just stay away from the bread and potatoes and rice for the first week, substitute carrots or celery, and concentrate on how great it will be not to have to worry about weight again. (And I mean never again. I'm willing to wager that if you stay on the diet six months you'll never go back to your old ways.) For those few people fortunate enough to be truly thin, French bread, English muffins, and other things of this sort may be added during this first week.

Incidentally, unbleached flour and brown rice are generally thought to be superior nutritionally. I also feel it is preferable to have a low sugar intake. For this reason, you won't find many desserts in the menus, as I hope you'll lose your craving for sweets when your body is fed by a balanced combination of foods. Moderation has never been one of my favorite words, but it's vitally important when applied to nutrition. Don't use too *much* margarine, don't drink too *much* coffee, don't use too *many* herbs! And above all, use salt sparingly. Generally speaking, a reduction of salt is found to be helpful. For those who must have salt for taste there is a product called Co Salt.

The following outline of a thirty-day plan is not intended to be followed meticulously and to the letter. It's quite likely it contains some foods you don't care for at all, and there may be some recipes too complicated for you to care to bother with. If there's something you particularly like, repeat it as often as you wish as a substitute for something else on the menu. For instance, for those who can't get fresh fish, the Tuna Casserole can be repeated. As to amounts, this must be left up to the discretion of the individual. A great strapping man who is going off to a hard day's work is obviously going to need more nourishment than a quiet elderly lady whose total game plan may be a walk around the block. Again, the magic word is moderation!

14

The One-Month Menu Plan

FIRST WEEK

First Day

Breakfast: Egg-White Omelet,* one thin piece
of French bread toast

Lunch: Tuna salad (½ can solid-pack white
tuna with chopped celery, green
onion, and safflower mayonnaise)

Dinner: Cup of hot clam juice generously
sprinkled with chopped parsley
Tuna Casserole I*
Green Beans

Second Day

Breakfast: Two medium stalks of celery stuffed
with a reasonable amount of peanut
butter

Lunch: Spinach-Shrimp Salad*

Dinner: Scalloped Oysters*
Steamed carrots
Braised Zucchini*
Small handful of walnuts (Walnuts
are high in polyunsaturates; other
nuts are all right depending on
allergies)

* Recipes to follow.

156

Third Day

Breakfast: Kippers, a thin piece of French
     bread toast

Lunch: Large bowl of vegetable soup
     (chopped vegetables cooked in chicken
     broth)

Dinner: Small green salad with oil, dill
     weed, and salt dressing
     Flounder Chinoise*
     Rice, with a dab of margarine
     ¼ head of cabbage, steamed with a
     dab of margarine

Fourth Day

Breakfast: Egg-White Omelet* made with
     herbs, a thin piece of toast

Lunch: Vegetable Tacos*

Dinner: Cup of chicken broth
     Brochette Provencal* (using frozen
     fish if necessary)
     Lima beans with sage
     Tiny handful of almonds

Fifth Day

Breakfast: 1 slice of French Toast,* with
     1 tablespoon of maple syrup

Lunch: Medium helping of Organic Salad*

Dinner: Sole, or Flounder, or Butterfish
     Meunière*
     Mixed squash (thin-sliced zucchini,
     yellow and acorn squash, cooked by
     pouring boiling water over and
     tossing)
     Dr. Dong's Basic Rice Pudding,* with
     brown sugar

Sixth Day

Breakfast: Egg-White Omelet* made with
                  green onions and parsley
Lunch: Gado Gado*
Dinner: Tuna Soufflé*
                 Fresh steamed spinach
                 Small baked potato, with a dab of
                     margarine
                 1 cookie
                 1 Almond Oatmeal Cookie*

Seventh Day

Breakfast: Chopped hard-boiled egg whites in a
                  thin White Sauce* on a piece of
                  thin toast
Lunch: Clam Chowder*
Dinner: Dr. Dong's Chicken*
                 Rice Pilaf with Vegetables*
                 1 peanut butter cookie

With the completion of the first week you should
begin to feel somewhat adjusted to the regime. Your
appetite should be satisfied; your general feeling
should be one of well-being, although it's too soon
to expect relief from the pains of arthritis. Since Dr.
Dong feels that thirty days is a reasonable test, you
must not feel discouraged if there's no relief sooner.
However, if at the end of a month's time there's no
relief *whatsoever,* it's probable that your problem has
other facets. The plan is, as I said, adjustable. If
there are foods not to your liking, substitute another
from the plan; if one doesn't agree with you for one
reason or another, try another. Portions should be
moderate, and always use a minimum of margarine.
And keep checking your weight.

SECOND WEEK

First Day

Breakfast: Dr. Dong's Basic Rice Pudding*
Lunch: Fish Aspic Salad,* with a few carrot
      sticks
Dinner: Corn Soup*
      Tuna Surprise*
      Sautéed eggplant

Second Day

Breakfast: Whole-grain cereal, melted marga-
      rine, and brown sugar
Lunch: Celery Victor,* sprinkled with
      hard-boiled egg white
Dinner: Small green salad with oil, dill weed,
      and garlic salt dressing
      Chicken Pie*
      Small serving of Angel Cream*

Third Day

Breakfast: English muffin, margarine, and raw
      honey
Lunch: Cooked vegetable salad
Dinner: Canned salmon loaf
      Brussels sprouts, small white boiling
      onions
      Rice
      A few walnuts

Fourth Day

Breakfast:	Egg-White Omelet* made with slivered green pepper, a thin piece of toast
Lunch:	Peanut butter and alfalfa sprout sandwich
Dinner:	Flounder Bonne Femme*
	Steamed carrots and peas
	Dr. Dong's Basic Rice Pudding,* with brown sugar

Fifth Day

Breakfast:	Creamed hard-boiled egg whites on thin toast
Lunch:	Leek and potato soup
Dinner:	Prawns sautéed in safflower oil and margarine
	Dollar Potatoes*
	Green Beans
	1 or 2 Sesame Seed Cookies*

Sixth Day

Breakfast:	1 Walnut Waffle,* with a tablespoon of maple syrup
Lunch:	Vegetables with Herbs*
Dinner:	Chicken with Broccoli*
	A small handful of walnuts (or other)

Seventh Day

Breakfast:	Kippers or sardines, a piece of toast
Lunch:	Clam Salad*
Dinner:	Half an avocado
	Tuna Casserole II*
	Spinach, small white boiling onions in White Sauce*
	1 Almond Oatmeal Cookie*

THIRD WEEK

First Day

Breakfast:	English muffin, with raw honey
Lunch:	Chinese Omelet*
Dinner:	Salad with mixed greens and raw vegetables
	Shellfish Soup*
	French bread, margarine

Second Day

Breakfast:	¼ can of tuna in thin White Sauce* on toast
Lunch:	Salade Niçoise*
Dinner:	Chicken in a Wok*
	Cold artichokes with safflower mayonnaise
	1 Sesame Seed Cookie*

Third Day

Breakfast:	French Toast,* with maple syrup
Lunch:	Alfalfa sprout and avocado sandwich
Dinner:	Steamed red snapper with soy-garlic-ginger sauce
	Baked Potato
	Green beans
	A handful of walnuts

Fourth Day

Breakfast: Pancakes,* with raw honey or syrup
Lunch: Shrimp salad with safflower mayon-
            naise
Dinner: Chicken Broth* with herbs and rice
            Tuna Pie*
            1 Almond Oatmeal Cookie*

Fifth Day

Breakfast: Corn bread
Lunch: Chicken sandwich
Dinner: Artichoke
            Sole or Flounder sautéed in oil and
                margarine, with chopped parsley
            Rice
            Creamed Spinach*

Sixth Day

Breakfast: Egg-White Omelet* made with sliv-
                ered celery
Lunch: Organic Salad*
Dinner: Bourride (Fish Stew)*
            Green salad

Seventh Day

Breakfast: Walnut Waffles with Syrup*
Lunch: Zucchini Fritatta*
Dinner: Cod with Mushrooms*
            Polenta*
            Broccoli

FOURTH WEEK

First Day

Breakfast: Dorothy's Arabic Bread,* marga-
           rine, and honey
Lunch: Steamed clams and broth
Dinner: Chicken Breasts Chinoise*
        Baked potato
        Creamed Cabbage*
        Small slice Mayonnaise Cake*

Second Day

Breakfast: Kippers, thin toast
Lunch: Crab and Rice Salad*
Dinner: Baked Haddock Steak*
        Rice with margarine and chopped
          parsley
        Fresh asparagus or green beans
        2 Macaroons*

Third Day

Breakfast: English muffin, with raw honey
Lunch: Fish Salad*
Dinner: Cold Cucumber Soup*
        Catfish Creole*
        Rice
        Green beans
        A few nuts

Fourth Day

Breakfast:	Egg-White Omelet* with slivered onions
Lunch:	Chicken sandwich, carrot sticks
Dinner:	Tuna Scrapple*
	Mixed green salad
	French bread
	Dr. Dong's Basic Rice Pudding,* with honey

Fifth Day

Breakfast:	¼ can tuna in thin White Sauce* on toast
Lunch:	Beat soup, a slice of French bread
Dinner:	Baked Shrimp*
	Sautéed green peppers
	Baked carrots

Sixth Day

Breakfast:	English muffin
Lunch:	Cold vegetable plate: boiled potato, beets, carrots, and zucchini, marinated together
Dinner:	Bourride (Fish Stew)*
	French bread
	Sabayon*

Seventh Day

Breakfast:	French Toast,* maple syrup
Lunch:	Chicken sandwich in Dorothy's Arabic Bread,* with safflower mayonnaise
Dinner:	Clam broth
	Tuna Casserole II*
	Baked potato
	Fresh spinach
	A few nuts

15

For Special Occasions

There are special occasions in everyone's life. The fact that you're coping with your arthritis through diet need not preclude your celebrating these occasions. The following menus are simply suggestions to stimulate your imagination. I'm sure you can fill in with items from the thirty-day plan, or perhaps you can improve on these menus with some inventions of your own.

I prefer to entertain no more than six or eight at a time, so my ideas for dinner parties are mainly geared to groups of this size. Obviously, the recipes are expandable, however.

Don't tell your guests they're eating an arthritic's diet *before* dinner. Wait till they've complimented you on a delicious repast, and then break the good news to them that they've had a healthful, nonfattening, cholesterol-free dinner.

BUFFET SUPPER FOR EIGHT OR TEN

To pass with the cocktails you don't drink:

Bowls of peanuts, walnuts, almonds

For special occasions

Herbed Toast*
Eggplant Caviar*
Grape Leaf Rolls*

On a tray as a first course:

Pass cups of Carrot and Tarragon Soup*

For dinner, arrange on the buffet:

Turkey Breast with Tuna Sauce on Rice*
Platter of cold cooked vegetables marinated in
oil, dill, and garlic salt: green beans, peas,
beets, zucchini, carrots, decorated with cocktail tomatoes and ripe olives
Long hot loaf of French bread, sliced and margarined
Carrot Cake*
Espresso Coffee

SMALL SEATED DINNER

With cocktails:

Shrimp Pâté* served with toast rounds

Dinner:

Chinese Eggdrop Soup*
Salmon en Croute*
Broccoli and baby carrots
French bread
Pecan Dessert*

SUNDAY NIGHT SUPPER

I particularly like Sunday nights. It's a nice informal time to entertain, and the food can be simple and
undemanding without sacrificing appeal. On Sunday
nights in winter I might serve Oyster Chowder* in big

earthenware bowls, a huge green salad, and lots of hot, crusty French bread. On a Sunday night in summer, when my crop of fresh basil is available (it's easy to grow in pots), I like to serve a big platter of spaghetti with Clam Pesto,* a green salad, crusty French bread, and Sabayon* for dessert. And, of course, coffee.

SUNDAY LUNCH

Sunday noon is a time we like to have people out from the city to lunch out-of-doors. I like to keep it simple and serve things that can be prepared ahead.

> Cold Cucumber Soup*
> Chicken Breasts Mary Elizabeth*
> Green salad
> Corn bread sticks
> Macaroons* and coffee

BIRTHDAY DINNER

> Fresh clams or oysters on the half shell
> Poached Salmon with Green Mayonnaise*
> Fresh asparagus
> Wild rice
> Angel Food Cake* and coffee

THANKSGIVING

It's fortunate that the white meat of turkey is allowable, for the rest of the turkey will be consumed by the others. I've found that everyone is just as happy with the following Thanksgiving dinner as they used to be with my more elaborate efforts.

> Smoked salmon on thin rye bread (I make my own)

Turkey with Oyster Dressing*
Mashed potatoes (mashed with just margarine
and a little broth)
Rutabaga (yellow turnip)—to satisfy my Wis-
consin heritage
Creamed tiny white onions—a must for my hus-
band
Pumpkin Chiffon Pie*

CHRISTMAS EVE

We like to have family and a few close friends in
for a big tureen of Oyster Stew,* a tradition with us on
Christmas Eve. I make an assortment of Christmas
cookies to munch while tree-trimming.

Italian Anise Cookies*
Sesame Seed Cookies*
Pfeffer Nuts*
Macaroons*

LADIES' BRIDGE PARTY

Poached Sole Chaudfroid*
Spinach-Stuffed Mushroom Caps*
Vanilla Soufflé*

A luncheon alternate might be Avocado Stuffed with
Chicken Salad.*

RECIPES

16

Basic Needs

CHICKEN BROTH

I make my chicken broth one of two ways: When I
poach chicken breasts, which I do fairly often to use
for chicken salad, sandwiches, or serving with a sauce,
I save the broth they were poached in. It is rich and
usually flavored with a little tarragon and perhaps a
bay leaf and some salt. The other way I make it is
by dropping a package of chicken legs in a pot, cov-
ering them well with water, and simmering till I feel
I've got all the chicken flavor I can out of the legs.
Here again I usually add a few herbs—bay leaf,

thyme, or marjoram—depending upon what I'm using the broth for. (I then throw away the legs because I've never thought of anything to do with them except tediously take the meat off the bones for the dog.)

COURT BOUILLON

This can be made ahead to be used for poaching fish. Chop a couple of carrots, a large celery stalk, and about 2 onions into a quart of water. Add a bay leaf, a good pinch of thyme, and several sprigs of parsley. Sea salt is a good addition to the flavor of fish, but it is rather hard to find. Simmer the mixture for about 30 minutes and strain before using. The addition of about a cup of white wine will improve this bouillon, but use it only after you really feel completely well.

FISH STOCK

Have the fish market give you the bones and trimmings when your fish is prepared. Put them in 1 quart of water with 1 sliced onion, a handful of parsley, salt (or sea salt), and simmer for about 30 minutes. Strain. Here again wine is a nice addition, but only if your arthritis is no longer giving you pain.

WHITE SAUCE

1 tablespoon margarine
1 tablespoon flour
1 cup chicken broth, clam juice, or water (depending on what you want to use the sauce with and what you have on hand).

Blend the margarine and flour over low heat to make a roux. Let it bubble a few minutes, then gradually add the chicken broth, clam juice, or water.

17

Breakfasts, Eggs, and Breads

FRENCH TOAST

Take a thin slice of French bread or regular bread made without eggs, butter, or additives. Soak in a slightly beaten egg white till moisture is absorbed, and brown in a small amount of safflower oil. (Or use a nonstick spray-on vegetable coating.) Serve with a thin pat of margarine and real maple syrup.

PANCAKES

1¼ cups flour	1 egg white
1 tablespoon sugar	1 cup water
1 tablespoon baking powder	2 tablespoons safflower oil
½ teaspoon salt	

Sift the dry ingredients together; beat the egg white lightly and add the other wet ingredients and mix thoroughly. Combine the wet and dry ingredients and stir just enough to mix together. The batter should be lumpy. Cook on an ungreased griddle or skillet.

WALNUT WAFFLES WITH SYRUP

1½ cups flour
2 teaspoons baking powder
½ teaspoon salt
1½ cups water

5 tablespoons safflower oil
2 egg whites, stiffly beaten
½ cup chopped walnuts

Sift the dry ingredients together, add the water and oil, and mix thoroughly till smooth. Fold in the stiffly beaten egg whites and pour the batter into a waffle iron that you have sprayed with a nonstick lecithin coating.

CHINESE OMELET

3 tablespoons chopped
    Chinese cabbage and/or
    bean sprouts
Safflower oil to cover bot-
    tom of pan

1 4½-ounce can shrimp, or
    equal amount fresh
    shrimp
5 egg whites
1 teaspoon cornstarch
Soy sauce
Pinch sugar

Sauté the vegetables slowly in the oil until just crisply tender; add the shrimp. Meanwhile, break the egg whites into a bowl. Do not beat them! Gently stir the vegetables into the egg whites in the bowl. When the mixture is well stirred, drop by the ladleful into the oiled pan, making small omelets about 6 inches across. Use a spatula to keep them from spreading; they will take form almost immediately. Cook them slowly till brown; turn and brown on the other side. Meanwhile put 1 teaspoon cornstarch in a bowl with a little cold water; add some soy sauce and a pinch of sugar; mix well. After the omelets are removed from the pan, pour this mixture into the pan and stir carefully till it becomes a clear, glazelike sauce to serve over the omelets.

EGG-WHITE OMELET

Heaping tablespoon slivered
green onion, celery, or
green pepper, or combina-
tion thereof
1 tablespoon safflower oil

2 egg whites per person
(give the yolks to the
dog)
Pinch salt

Sauté the vegetable of your choice lightly in the oil,
preferably using a Teflon pan. This will take a very
short time. Remove the vegetables from the oil with
a slotted spoon, stir into the egg whites, and add salt.
Do not beat; just stir around gently to mix. Slide the
mixture into the still-hot pan and sauté a very short
time, just enough to brown lightly. Turn, brown, and
serve. You can make this in any number of variations;
I'm very fond of onions and often make an omelet
with lots of sliced mild onions for a luncheon dish.

BRAN ENGLISH MUFFINS

1 square yeast, dissolved in
¼ cup lukewarm water
(be sure your yeast is
fresh)
1 cup very warm water
1 teaspoon salt
2 teaspoons honey (op-
tional—I prefer without)

1 heaping cup bran
2 cups stone-ground whole-
wheat flour
2 cups unbleached white
flour
3 tablespoons soft marga-
rine

Combine the dissolved yeast, water, salt, honey, and
bran in a large bowl. Mix the flours together in a separate bowl, and gradually beat half of the flour into
the bran mixture. Cover the bowl and allow to rise in
a warm place for 1½ hours. Beat in the margarine
and add the rest of the flour, reserving ½ cup for the
board. Turn out onto the board and knead until
smooth. Don't skimp on the kneading! Pat the dough
out, spreading till it's about ¾ inch thick. Cut into

3-inch rounds; cover on the board for about 1 hour. Cook, at a preheated 300 degrees, in an electric fry pan or on the griddle of your stove, lightly oiled, for 12 or 13 minutes, turning once. If you don't have either of these, use an iron griddle. To serve, split and toast.

DOROTHY'S ARABIC BREAD

5½ cups unbleached wheat flour
½ cup stone-ground whole-wheat flour

½ teaspoon salt
2½ cups water
2 packages dry yeast
3 tablespoons safflower oil

Sift together the flours and salt. Heat the 2½ cups of water to 110 degrees (you'll have to guess if you haven't a thermometer). Pour some of the warm water into a large mixing bowl and add the 2 packages of dry yeast and the 3 tablespoons of safflower oil. Alternately add the flour and water. Mix well and knead on a bread board for about 10 minutes. Let rise in a warm place for 1½ hours, then roll out like a long jelly roll, and slice into 14 equal parts. Take each piece and roll it out ¾ inch thick. Place each piece on a 4x4-inch square of foil, and let rise for another hour. Preheat the oven to 500 degrees, brush each piece with oil, and bake 9 minutes on the lowest rack in the oven. (You can probably bake 4 at a time.)

WHOLE-WHEAT BREAD

2 teaspoons salt
2 tablespoons margarine
2 cups warm water
1 square yeast, dissolved in ¼ cup lukewarm water

2½ cups unsifted all-purpose flour (unbleached)
3 cups unsifted stone-ground whole-wheat flour (I use Stone-Buhr)

Mix the salt and margarine with the warm water. Add the yeast and the all-purpose flour. Start adding the whole-wheat flour slowly, and when all is mixed in, turn out onto a floured board. Knead until the dough is smooth and elastic, from 5 to 10 minutes. Place in an oiled bowl, cover with a dish towel, and place in a pan of hot water in an unlighted oven for about 1½ hours. It should double in bulk. Knead again, and let rise again in the same way. Shape into 2 loaves and place in 2 oiled 9x5-inch loaf pans. Let rise once again till double in size. Bake at 400 degrees for 45 minutes. Let cool on a wire rack.

18

Appetizers

GRAPE LEAF ROLLS

2 or 3 onions, finely
  chopped
1 cup mixed white and wild
  rice
8 green onions, chopped
½ cup chopped parsley

2 tablespoons dill weed
5 or 6 tablespoons finely
  chopped walnuts
½ cup olive oil mixed with
  ½ cup water
Canned grape leaves

Sauté the onions in a little olive oil, then mix together
all the ingredients, except the grape leaves, and simmer for about 10 minutes. Rinse the leaves carefully
to remove the brine. Wrap each leaf around 1 teaspoon
(approximately) of the rice mixture and put them in
a large skillet in 1 layer. Pour over them about ½ cup
of olive oil mixed with ½ cup of water. Put a
heavy lid over the rolls to keep them from unwrap-
ping, and simmer for 45 minutes.

EGGPLANT CAVIAR

1 green pepper, seeded and
  chopped
1 onion, chopped
3 tablespoons olive oil

1 clove garlic, crushed
1 baked eggplant, pared and
  seeded
Salt to taste

Sauté the green pepper and onion in the olive oil; add the garlic and eggplant. Salt to taste, and serve with crisp, thin wedges of toasted French bread.

HERBED TOAST

Chop equal parts of parsley, tarragon, and chives very fine. Mix with ½ cup of margarine and spread on very thin slices of French bread, preferably from one of the long, thin loaves. Toast in a 350-degree oven till brown and crisp.

SHRIMP PÂTÉ

Put ½ pound of small cooked shrimp in the blender with ½ cup olive oil. Puree, then add another cup of oil, salt to taste, and a dash of paprika. Refrigerate covered. Serve on a platter with melba toast points. This recipe makes quite a lot but you can adjust for a smaller amount easily.

19

Soups

BOURRIDE (FISH STEW)

1 onion, chopped
2 tablespoons olive oil
2 leeks, chopped
3 carrots, sliced
1 celery heart, chopped
¼ cup chopped parsley
3 potatoes, peeled and sliced
1 pound cod fillets (or whatever firm-fleshed fish is available)

2 cups hot fish stock (see page 170)
1 tablespoon white wine (optional)
Salt to taste
Slices of French bread
Cooking oil
Margarine
1 cup mayonnaise mixed with 1 garlic clove, crushed.

Sauté the chopped onion in the olive oil, add the rest of the vegetables, and stir over low heat for 5 minutes. Place the fish on top of the vegetables, cover tightly, and simmer over very low heat for 30 minutes or until the vegetables are tender. Remove the fish to a warm platter, pour the vegetables into a blender, and puree till smooth. Pour the puree into a tureen, add the hot fish stock slowly, plus 1 tablespoon of white wine if you wish, and season to taste with salt. Place slices of French bread that have been sautéed in a little oil and margarine in the bottom of each soup bowl, place a piece of fish on it, pour over the soup, and top with a spoonful of mayonnaise that's been mixed with a crushed clove of garlic.

CARROT AND TARRAGON SOUP

½ stick margarine
1½ pounds carrots, scraped
and chopped
1 medium potato, peeled
and chopped

1 medium onion, chopped
2 pints chicken broth
½ teaspoon dried tarragon
Salt

Melt the margarine and stir in the vegetables. Cover and cook for 10 minutes. Add the broth and the seasonings, simmer for about 25 minutes, and put through a blender. Serve either hot or cold.

CLAM CHOWDER

1 onion, chopped
2 stalks celery, chopped
½ small eggplant, peeled
and diced
1 tablespoon safflower oil
1 tablespoon margarine

1 8-ounce can minced
clams, drained (reserve
juice)
2 cups water
½ teaspoon basil
Salt to taste
Chopped parsley

Sauté the onion, celery, and eggplant in the oil and margarine. When tender, add the drained-off clam juice, 2 cups of water, the basil, and salt to taste. Cover and simmer for about 30 minutes. Add the clams, run in a blender for 30 seconds, and serve. This chowder is a rather unattractive gray color because of the eggplant, so it helps to sprinkle it very generously with chopped parsley.

COLD CUCUMBER SOUP

¼ cup chopped onion
2 tablespoons safflower oil
2 cups diced cucumber
1 cup watercress
½ cup finely diced raw
potato

2 cups chicken broth
2 sprigs parsley
½ teaspoon salt
Snipped chives

Cook the onion in the oil until transparent. Add the remaining ingredients and bring to a boil. Reduce the heat and simmer about 15 minutes. When the potatoes are tender, puree in a blender and chill. Serve topped with snipped chives.

CORN SOUP

1 17-ounce can creamed corn	¼ teaspoon sesame oil
4 cups chicken broth	Salt to taste
2 tablespoons sherry	1 egg white, stiffly beaten

Combine all ingredients except the egg white in a saucepan and bring to a boil. Simmer gently for about 2 minutes, then fold in the stiffly beaten egg white and serve immediately.

DR. DONG'S MAGIC MIXTURE

This is to be carried in a thermos, hot! It's fine for a football game, a winter outing, or anything of that sort, but it is actually what Dr. Dong takes to his office every day of his life. It's sustaining, perfect nourishment, and he makes it himself every morning!

Put about a cup or so of leftover cooked rice in a blender, add a cooked vegetable such as carrots (this depends on your taste—I like onion and carrots) and ½ can of tuna, or you can use breast of chicken. Add 2 cups of water, a little salt, and blend thoroughly. Put it in a pan, add another cup of water, and heat it to the boiling point. Then add about ½ tablespoon of safflower oil and put the mixture into the thermos. Dr. Dong drinks a cup of this about every 2 hours while he's in his office; I think it explains how he maintains his backbreaking schedule. This concoction could very well be the answer for those who carry a lunch to work.

CHINESE EGGDROP SOUP

1 tablespoon cornstarch
3 cups chicken broth
1 egg white

1 green onion, chopped,
    top and all
1 teaspoon salt

Dissolve the cornstarch in 3 tablespoons of the cold broth; heat the remaining broth to boiling and add the cornstarch mixture, stirring. Beat the egg white with a fork, and slowly pour into the broth. Add the salt, stir once lightly and remove from the heat; serve with green onion sprinkled on top.

OYSTER CHOWDER

1 medium onion, finely
    chopped
2 cloves garlic, crushed
3 tablespoons margarine
1 package frozen chopped
    spinach

½ pound fresh mushrooms,
    washed and sliced
2½ cups chicken broth
¼ teaspoon basil
¼ teaspoon oregano
1 pint oysters
Salt to taste

Sauté the onion and garlic in 1 tablespoon of the margarine in a Dutch oven or similar heavy pot. Add the spinach and mushrooms, cover, and cook till the spinach is thawed, stirring often. Add the chicken broth, herbs, and the oysters and their liquor. (Cut the oysters into bite-sized pieces if necessary.) Heat only up to the boiling point, salt to taste, and stir in the other 2 tablespoons of margarine. Serve at once.

OYSTER STEW

1 pint oysters
½ cup finely chopped celery
¼ cup margarine
3 cups chicken stock

1 small potato, boiled in a
    little water and pureed in
    a blender
Salt to taste
Chopped parsley

Cook the oysters and celery in the margarine about 3 minutes. Add 1 cup of the chicken stock and work in the pureed potato as a thickener. Add the rest of the chicken stock, salt to taste, sprinkle with the chopped parsley, and serve piping hot.

SHELLFISH SOUP

1 tablespoon olive oil	½ teaspoon basil
1 tablespoon safflower oil	½ teaspoon thyme
1 large onion, chopped fine	Few threads saffron
1 clove garlic, crushed	2 dozen clams
2 carrots, chopped fine	1 pound medium shrimp,
5 cups chicken broth	shelled and deveined
3 8-ounce bottles clam juice	1 10-ounce jar small oysters
¼ cup dry vermouth	

Heat the olive and safflower oil, add the onion, garlic, and carrots, and sauté till tender. Add the chicken broth, clam juice, vermouth, basil, thyme, and saffron, and simmer for about 30 minutes. Let cool, and refrigerate for at least 24 hours. When ready to serve, reheat the broth to boiling, and add the clams, shrimp, and oysters. Cover. Reduce heat and simmer till clams open, about 8 minutes. This will serve 6 generously—ask some friends in!

20

Salads

AVOCADO STUFFED WITH CHICKEN SALAD

Mix together: diced, cooked chicken breasts, diced celery and cucumber, chopped green onion, and safflower mayonnaise. Serve in an avocado half on lettuce leaves.

CELERY VICTOR

Scrape and trim celery stalks into uniform lengths, discarding the tougher parts. Cover with water, add ¼ cup of soy sauce, and simmer till tender. Marinate in safflower oil and salt.

CHEF'S SALAD BOWL

Wash and thoroughly dry salad greens. Add a handful of small shrimp, some white meat of chicken cut in matchstick strips, some slivers of green peppers, a good amount of chopped celery and green onion, and a hard-boiled egg white. Dress with oil, garlic salt, and a little dill weed.

CLAM SALAD

1 8-ounce can chopped (not minced) clams
Several stalks tender celery, diced
3 scallions, with a little of the green top
About ¼ green pepper, cut in slivers
Safflower mayonnaise
Lettuce leaves

Drain the clams, but not completely—retain a little of their juice. Mix the celery, scallions, and green pepper together with just enough mayonnaise to hold them together, and season to taste. Serve on crisp lettuce.

CRAB AND RICE SALAD

1 8-ounce can crabmeat
1¼ cups cooked, chilled rice
⅓ cup chopped celery
2 green onions, chopped
¼ cup sliced water chestnuts
½ teaspoon soy sauce
½ cup mayonnaise
Lettuce leaves

Mix together all the ingredients, except the lettuce, and chill well. Serve in crisp lettuce nests.

FISH ASPIC SALAD

2 envelopes unflavored gelatin
1 cup cold water
1¾ cups cold chicken broth
1 tablespoon liquid from pimento-stuffed olives
⅛ teaspoon salt
1 cup flaked cooked fish (sole, halibut, etc.)
2 tablespoons chopped pimento-stuffed olives
Salad greens and watercress

Dissolve the gelatin in the water and cook over low heat for about 5 minutes, stirring constantly. Remove from the heat, add the chicken broth, olive liquid, and salt, and chill till the mixture thickens slightly. Fold in the fish and chopped olives, turn into a 4-cup mold, and chill until firm. Unmold on the salad greens.

FISH SALAD

1 pound firm white fish
(such as turbot),
poached, drained, and
chilled
¼ cup chopped onion
¼ cup chopped parsley

1 large bay leaf, finely
crumbled
About ⅓ cup olive oil
Salt to taste
Slivered celery root

Cut the fish into bite-sized pieces; marinate with dressing made from the onion, parsley, bay leaf, olive oil, and salt. Serve slivered celery root on the side.

ORGANIC SALAD

2 cups shredded cabbage
1½ cups fresh bean sprouts
1 cup shredded carrots
½ cup alfalfa sprouts
1 tablespoon olive oil
1½ tablespoons mayon-
naise
1 tablespoon maple syrup

½ tablespoon dried cilantro
leaves (coriander)
½ tablespoon dried green
onions
Salt to taste
Dash of garlic powder
(optional)

Mix all ingredients together and chill in refrigerator. This salad will keep several days.

SALADE NICOISE

New potatoes, boiled whole
in their jackets
Green beans, cooked crisp
Beets, cooked or canned
Tuna (the best solid-packed
white albacore)
Lettuce leaves

Anchovies
Black olives
1 clove garlic crushed in
½ cup olive oil
Touch dry mustard
Good dash salt

Chill the boiled potatoes, cooked green beans, cooked beets, and tuna, and arrange on a bed of lettuce in the desired proportions. Decorate with strips of anchovies and black olives. Crush 1 clove of garlic in ½ cup of olive oil, add a touch of dry mustard (just the merest whisper), and a good dash of salt, and pour over the salad.

SPINACH-SHRIMP SALAD

Wash tender young spinach leaves and dry carefully. Add shrimp and chopped, hard-boiled egg whites. Toss lightly with safflower oil mixed with a little olive oil and seasoned with garlic salt.

21

Spaghetti Sauces

CLAM PESTO

4 cloves garlic, crushed (cut
    this amount down if you
    don't like garlic as much
    as I do)
4 tablespoons olive oil
4 8-ounce cans chopped
    clams (reserve the liquid)

½ cup white wine
1 pound spaghetti
½ stick margarine
1 cup finely chopped fresh
    basil

Cook the garlic briefly in the olive oil, add the liquid
from the clams and the wine, and simmer for at least
30 minutes. Cook the spaghetti in plenty of boiling
water, drain off all the water but ½ cup, and add
½ stick of margarine. Add the clams and basil to
the reduced sauce, heat through, and serve over the
spaghetti.

PESTO

2 cups fresh basil
½ cup olive oil
2 tablespoons pine nuts
2 cloves garlic, crushed

1 teaspoon salt
3 tablespoons margarine (at
    room temperature)

Grind the basil with the oil in a mortar until you have a paste. Add the pine nuts and grind them into the paste. When it is all smooth, add the other ingredients. Serve over spaghetti.

22

Fish

BROCHETTE PROVENÇAL

1 1-pound firm white fish
  (flounder, bass, sole, etc.)
8 large shrimp
8 scallops

Flour
2 egg whites, slightly beaten
½ teaspoon salt
1 tablespoon safflower oil

Cut the fish into eight pieces and arrange the sea-food alternately on four skewers. Roll them in flour, then in a mixture of 2 slightly beaten egg whites, ½ teaspoon salt, and 1 tablespoon of safflower oil. Sauté in a large saucepan in safflower oil, or barbecue over charcoal.

CATFISH CREOLE

½ pound catfish fillets,
  fresh or frozen
2 tablespoons flour
1 tablespoon margarine
1 tablespoon safflower oil
¼ cup water
½ cup sliced celery
¼ cup sliced green onions
  with tops

¼ cup chopped green
  pepper
1 clove garlic, crushed
1 cup white sauce
1 bay leaf
¼ teaspoon thyme
2 tablespoons chopped
  parsley
Hot, cooked rice

Thaw the fish if frozen, and cut into 1-inch pieces. Brown the flour in the margarine and oil, remove from the heat, and cool slightly. Add the water gradually and stir till blended. Add everything else except the fish and rice, cover, and simmer for 20 minutes or until the vegetables are tender. Remove the bay leaf, add the catfish, and simmer for 10 minutes longer or until the fish flakes easily when fork-tested. Serve over the rice.

CATFISH WITH HERBS

1 3-pound catfish
Salt
1 tablespoon chervil
1 tablespoon fresh tarragon, or ½ teaspoon dried
1 teaspoon dried fennel
2 large stalks celery, cut in strips
1 onion, minced
Several lettuce leaves
¼ pound mushrooms, chopped quite fine
1 clove garlic, crushed
½ cup oil
¼ pound margarine

Skin the fish by grasping the skin at the top of the spine and pulling it right down the back. It has no scales and will come away quite easily. Salt the insides and stuff with the herbs, celery, and onion. Place the fish in a baking dish and cover with lettuce leaves that have been dipped in boiling water. Sauté the mushrooms and garlic in the oil and margarine, pour over the fish, and bake for about 30 minutes or until the fish flakes with a fork. Remove the fish to a hot platter, reduce the remaining juices somewhat, and pour over the fish.

CATFISH MARTIGUES

½ onion, sliced
2 cloves garlic, crushed
2 canned anchovies, well rinsed in hot water
1 2½-pound catfish
Salt
¾ cup fish stock or water
2 tablespoons white wine
1 tablespoon flour
1 tablespoon olive oil
1 tablespoon margarine

Mix the onion, garlic, and achovies and place in the bottom of an oiled baking dish. Place the fish on this bed, salt very lightly, moisten with the stock (or water) and wine, and bake at 350 degrees for about 25 minutes. In another pan, blend the flour into the olive oil and brown slightly. After the fish has been removed to a serving platter, pour the juices from the baking dish into the flour-oil roux and beat with a wire whisk. Cook over low heat for a few minutes, beating, then beat in the margarine and serve with the fish.

COD WITH MUSHROOMS

1 cup chopped celery
2 tablespoons chopped chives
1 cup chicken broth
1 pound cod or haddock fillets

Salt
Paprika
½ cup sliced mushrooms
2 teaspoons margarine

Cook the celery and chives in the chicken broth for about 5 minutes, then puree in a blender. Place the fish fillets in an oiled baking dish, sprinkle with a little salt and paprika, pour over the celery mixture and bake at 400 degrees for about 15 minutes.

FLOUNDER BONNE FEMME

¼ pound fresh mushrooms, chopped
1 tablespoon minced shallot
3 tablespoons minced parsley

Salt to taste
1½ pounds flounder fillets
1 cup court bouillon
2 tablespoons margarine
Parsley sprigs

Mix together the mushrooms, shallot, and parsley, and spread on the bottom of a margarined shallow casserole or pan. Salt the fillets, arrange them on the mushrooms, and pour the court bouillon over all.

Cook about 20 minutes in a 350-degree oven. Remove the fillets, keeping them warm while you reduce the sauce to about 1 cup. Add 2 tablespoons of margarine and pour over the flounder. Garnish with parsley sprigs and serve.

FLOUNDER CHINOISE

This recipe was given me over the counter by Merle Ellis, San Francisco's famous butcher/television personality/columnist/cook. It is simple Chinese-style cooking at its best, delicious and easy to prepare.

Take fillets of flounder, the number depending on their size, and poach them in a small amount of water in which you've sliced thinly some fresh ginger root. They will only need to poach about 3 or 4 minutes; test with a fork for flaking. Remove the fish from the water, place on a serving dish, and sprinkle with chopped green onions and some thin slices of ginger root as a garnish. Heat some sesame oil and pour it and a small amount of soy sauce over the fish and serve.

BAKED HADDOCK OR
HALIBUT STEAK

If possible, get your fish man to bone a nice piece of haddock or halibut. If this is not possible, you can cook it with the bones in—it's just nice to have them out of the way. Lay the fish in an ovenproof dish on a bed of onions, parsley, and green pepper, and if it's boned, put the vegetables between the two pieces. Pour a little safflower oil over and around the fish, and bake in a preheated 350-degree oven for about 40 minutes for 2 to 3 lbs., for 1½ hours for a whole fish. Baste from time to time with fish stock. If you like, you can add a handful of shrimp about 10 minutes before it's done.

SCALLOPED OYSTERS

2 glass jars (about 10 ounces each) fresh oysters
¼ cup melted margarine

2 cups French bread crumbs
Salt

Drain the oysters and dry them carefully on paper towels. Dip each oyster into the melted margarine; then roll it in the bread crumbs till completely covered. Lay the oysters in a casserole, salting them rather generously, and bake in a 350-degree oven for 30 minutes.

POACHED SALMON WITH GREEN MAYONNAISE

This can be done either with a large fillet of salmon or the desired number of salmon steaks. Bring enough court bouillon, to cover, to a simmer in a shallow pan, and slide the salmon in. Maintain the heat evenly at a simmer; watch the salmon carefully because it cooks quickly and is best when a trifle underdone. Lift from the bouillon with a slotted spoon, drain carefully, and place on a heated platter.

Serve with the following sauce: Drop a handful of spinach leaves, a small handful of watercress leaves, and a small handful of parsley sprigs in boiling water for just a minute. Drain well in paper towels, and chop very, very fine. Stir into 2 cups of safflower mayonnaise.

SALMON EN CROUTE

This is one of my favorites. It's impressive, not hard to do, and absolutely delicious. An ideal way to use salmon is to entertain twice with it. I bake it the first time, serving only the top half—in other words, serving off the bone. Then, depending on when I plan to use the other half, I either freeze it or refrigerate it. When I'm ready to use it, I carefully remove the bone; the spine will usually come away in one piece when it's cold. I also remove the skin. Then I'm ready to prepare my Salmon en Croute. If you wish, however, you can start out with a large fillet of salmon, or even a small whole salmon, and bone it after cooking. In any case, we now have a good-sized piece of cooked salmon.

Make a pastry as for Chicken Pie (see page 202); when chilled, divide it in half. Roll out half of the pastry in the shape of the salmon, a long, narrow piece extending slightly beyond the outline of the salmon. Place the piece of pastry on an ovenproof platter and lay the fish carefully on it. (It takes a bit of doing not to break it, but if you do, you can piece it together.) Now arrange on the fish ½ cup of rice cooked in clam juice with a little tarragon. Sprinkle this with chopped hard-boiled egg whites and chopped parsley. Roll out the other half of the pastry, allowing enough extra for the mound of the fish, and place on top. Wet the edges with a pastry brush and crimp with a fork. Make one or two slits in the top, and pour in a large amount of melted margarine—½ stick for a good-sized fish. Bake in a preheated 400-degree oven until the pastry is lightly browned.

To serve, slice down through the layers of rice and fish, and pass a bowl of mayonnaise thinned down with a little clam juice and a tiny bit of white wine.

SHISH KEBAB

Scallops	Olive oil
Prawns	1 garlic clove, crushed
Green peppers, cut in hunks	1 bay leaf
Quartered onions	Tarragon
Large whole mushrooms	Oregano

Use both scallops and prawns or one or the other, allowing about 4 items per person. Marinate the fish and vegetables in olive oil, crushed garlic, a bay leaf, about a teaspoon each tarragon and oregano. Thread on skewers and barbecue or broil.

BAKED SHRIMP

5 tablespoons margarine	3 cups hot, cooked rice
5 tablespoons flour	½ cup chopped parsley
2 cups chicken broth	½ cup sliced green onions,
1 teaspoon salt	tops and all
Few tablespoons dry sherry	2½ cups cooked shrimp

Melt the margarine, and add the flour to make a roux. Slowly add the chicken broth, and stir till the sauce thickens. Add the remaining ingredients and turn into a shallow baking dish. Bake about 20 minutes in a 350-degree oven.

POACHED SOLE CHAUDFROID

4 even-sized sole fillets (you might substitute flounder, although the flavor is not quite so delicate)	2 tablespoons gelatin
	2 cups safflower mayonnaise
Court bouillon flavored with tarragon	Watercress sprigs

Cover the sole with the court bouillon; reduce the heat and simmer very gently until nearly done. At this point, remove the pan from the stove and let the sole finish cooking in the broth. When the broth is cool, carefully remove the sole and arrange it on a serving dish. Soften the gelatin in ½ cup of the broth; dissolve over hot water. Blend in 2 cups of safflower mayonnaise, and chill. When the mayonnaise mixture is thickened, but not jelled, pour over the fish to mask it. This thickening process should take about ½ hour. Watch it carefully—once it jells, you've had it! Remove the fish from the refrigerator about ½ hour ahead of serving so it won't be too cold. Garnish with watercress.

SOLE, FLOUNDER, OR BUTTER
FISH MEUNIÈRE

2 tablespoons safflower oil	Flour
2 tablespoons margarine	Salt
4 small fillets of sole, flounder, or butterfish	Chopped parsley

Heat the oil and margarine in a heavy skillet, dust the fillets with flour, salt lightly, and sauté in the hot oil and margarine till lightly browned, turning once. (About 2 minutes to a side should be enough.) Transfer to a hot platter, add the chopped parsley to the oil and margarine in the pan, stir, and pour over the fish.

TUNA CASSEROLE I

½ stick margarine	2 7-ounce cans white tuna (albacore)
1 smallish onion, chopped	French bread crumbs
2 tablespoons flour	
1½ cups clam juice	

Melt the margarine and sauté the onion. Gradually work in the flour to make a smooth mixture; add the clam juice gradually and stir till thick. Pour this over the tuna in a shallow casserole and top with French bread crumbs. Bake in a 350-degree oven for 20 minutes.

TUNA CASSEROLE II

½ onion, chopped
¼ green pepper, sliced thin
1 tablespoon safflower oil
1 tablespoon margarine
1 tablespoon flour
1 cup chicken broth

Heaping tablespoon sliced
  canned pimentos
Salt
1 8-ounce can solid-pack
  tuna
Paprika

Sauté the onion and green pepper in the oil and margarine. Pull them to one side of the pan, work the flour into the remaining oil and margarine, and simmer, stirring, 1 or 2 minutes. Slowly add the broth and stir till thickened and creamy. Add the pimentos, a little salt, and pour over the tuna in a shallow baking dish. Sprinkle with a few dashes of paprika and bake in a 350-degree oven for 20 minutes.

TUNA PIE

2 carrots, diced
1 large potato, diced
1 large onion, chopped
1 8-ounce can solid-pack
  tuna, flaked

¾ cup white sauce (see
  recipe for Tuna Surprise,
  page 199)
Biscuit dough (see below)

Cook the vegetables in a little boiling water till just tender; drain and mix with the tuna and white sauce in an oiled baking dish. Cover with biscuit dough and bake 20 minutes at 375 degrees.

Biscuit Dough:

Sift 1 cup of flour with 1½ teaspoons of baking powder; cut in 2 tablespoons of margarine and add about ⅓ cup of water. Mix well and add a little more water if necessary. Turn out on a lightly floured board and form into a smooth ball; roll out to a ¼-inch thickness and place on the Tuna Pie.

TUNA SCRAPPLE

1 cup yellow cornmeal
1 teaspoon salt
1 cup cold water
3 cups scalded fish stock
1 8-ounce can tuna, drained

1 egg white, slightly beaten
Flour
Safflower oil
Margarine

Mix the cornmeal, salt, and cold water in the top of a double boiler. Gradually stir in the fish stock and cook over hot water for about 2 hours, stirring frequently. Stir in the tuna and continue cooking for another 20 minutes, stirring occasionally. Pour into 2 greased loaf pans, cover, and refrigerate. When cold and firm, slice thin. Dip first in the beaten egg white, then in flour, and brown on both sides in oil and margarine.

TUNA SOUFFLÉ

1 tablespoon flour
1 tablespoon margarine
⅔ cup water
½ cup soft bread crumbs
2 cups tuna, flaked

1 teaspoon chopped parsley
1 teaspoon chopped chives
1 teaspoon onion juice
Salt
3 egg whites, well beaten

Make a cream sauce by blending 1 tablespoon flour with 1 tablespoon margarine, cooking and stirring till creamy smooth. Add ⅔ cup water slowly, and stir, cooking till smooth. Add the bread crumbs and continue cooking for a few minutes, then add the rest of the ingredients and mix well. Lastly, fold in the well-beaten egg whites and bake in a 400-degree oven for about 25 minutes. Chopped, sautéed mushrooms are good served with this dish.

TUNA SURPRISE

1 onion, finely chopped	2 cups chicken broth
1 tablespoon safflower oil	2 8-ounce cans tuna
3 tablespoons margarine	Small package potato chips,
2 tablespoons flour	crumbled

Brown 1 finely chopped onion in the oil and 1 table-spoon of margarine. Make a white sauce by mixing 2 tablespoons flour with 2 tablespoons margarine, cooking a minute or two, and gradually adding 2 cups of chicken broth. Flake the tuna and put in layers in a baking dish, alternating the tuna, white sauce, and a small package of crumbled potato chips. Bake for 20 minutes at 350 degrees.

23

Chicken

BAKED CHICKEN WITH HERBS

6 chicken breasts
5 tablespoons olive oil and
safflower oil, mixed half
and half
½ teaspoon each thyme,
basil, and marjoram

1 tablespoon fresh-cut
chives
Flour
Salt
1 cup water
1 tablespoon minced parsley

Wipe the chicken breasts with a damp cloth. Place in
a bowl and pour 3 tablespoons of oil over them; sprinkle with the mixed herbs and chives. Cover and let
stand in the refrigerator for 3 or 4 hours. Lift the
chicken from the marinade, dust lightly with flour, and
brown 15 minutes in 2 tablespoons of the oil. Arrange
the breasts in a large, shallow casserole in 1 layer;
sprinkle lightly with salt. Mix the marinade remaining
in the bowl with 1 cup of water; add the parsley to it
and pour this over the chicken. Cover and bake in a
375-degree oven for 30 minutes. Uncover periodically
to see if the chicken is done; baste frequently with the
marinade in the casserole.

CHICKEN BREASTS CHINOISE

Place two skinned chicken breasts in a shallow pan.
Mix 2 tablespoons of soy sauce with 2 tablespoons of

sesame oil, ½ teaspoon of salt, and ¼ teaspoon of ginger. Brush this mixture on the chicken and bake uncovered for about 45 minutes at 350 degrees.

CHICKEN BREASTS MARY ELIZABETH

2 chicken breasts, skinned
and boned
1 egg white, slightly beaten
1 cup bread crumbs
Safflower oil

1 cup chicken broth
1 tablespoon cornstarch
Small pinch curry powder
Pinch salt

Dip the chicken in the egg white, then roll in the bread crumbs. Sauté in about ¼ inch of safflower oil. Place in a baking dish, pour over 1 cup of chicken broth thickened with 1 tablespoon of cornstarch and seasoned with a pinch of curry powder and salt. Bake for 20 minutes in a 350-degree oven.

CHICKEN IN A WOK

A wok is a Chinese cooking utensil, a metal pan shaped like a bowl that holds heat uniformly over its surface and cooks quickly and evenly. It isn't essential that you have one; you can prepare this in your old iron skillet. But woks are good for this sort of cooking and fun to use.

1 large chicken breast,
boned and cut in 2½ x
2½-inch strips
½ teaspoon powdered
ginger
¼ teaspoon salt
Dash paprika
1 tablespoon safflower oil

¾ cup diagonally sliced
celery
¼ cup sliced green pepper
¼ cup chopped green onion
1 cup chicken broth
1 tablespoon soy sauce
½ tablespoon cornstarch
mixed with a little cold
water

Mix the chicken with the ginger, salt, and paprika. Heat the oil in the wok and sauté the chicken for about 5 minutes, stirring frequently. Push the chicken aside, add the vegetables, and cook for about 5 minutes longer, stirring frequently. Add the broth and the soy sauce, cover, and cook on low heat for another 5 minutes. Stir in the cornstarch, cook till the sauce thickens slightly, and serve.

CHICKEN PIE

Pastry:

¾ stick margarine
1 cup flour
Large pinch salt

2 to 3 tablespoons cold
    water
1 egg white, slightly beaten

Break the margarine up into bits and add to the dry ingredients. Mix with your hands till blended, and add enough water to allow you to make the dough into a ball. Refrigerate for an hour before rolling out.

Filling:

6 or 8 chicken breasts
    (skinned)
1½ quarts chicken broth
About 10 small white
    boiling onions
2 carrots, scraped and
    sliced lengthwise

¼ pound mushrooms
⅓ cup flour
½ stick margarine
¼ teaspoon salt
1 or 2 dozen oysters
    (optional)

Cover the chicken with the broth, bring to a boil, and simmer till tender. Remove the chicken from the broth and skim any scum from the surface of the broth. Add the onions and carrots and simmer for 10 minutes; add the mushrooms and cook until the vegetables are tender. Remove them from the broth. While they are cooking, remove the chicken meat from the bones, cutting it into serving-sized pieces. Make a cream sauce of the flour, margarine, and 3 cups of the broth. Salt, mix with the chicken and vegetables, and pour into a baking dish. Top with the pastry, make a few slits for steam, brush with the slightly beaten egg white, and bake for 45 minutes at 350 degrees. The addition of 1 or 2 dozen oysters, depending on size, to this pie makes a delightful combination of flavors.

CHICKEN WITH BROCCOLI

Slightly undercook 1 bunch of broccoli, and arrange it in the bottom of a casserole. Poach 3 boned chicken breasts in water to barely cover, reserving 1½ cups of the resulting broth. Brown the breasts in a little oil and margarine, arrange on the broccoli, and pour a sauce made from mixing the 1½ cups of chicken broth with ½ cup of safflower mayonnaise, ½ teaspoon of cilantro (coriander), and a very slight pinch of curry powder. Bake only about 15 or 20 minutes at 350 degrees.

DR. DONG'S CHICKEN

Wash and dry 1 whole roasting chicken and lightly salt. Make a paste of 2 tablespoons of brown sugar and 2 tablespoons of thick soy sauce. (If you cannot find the thick soy sauce, use the regular, but check the label carefully for MSG and additives.) Cover the chicken with about half the paste and put into the oven on a rack. Cook for 30 minutes at 400 degrees. Baste with the remaining sugar and soy sauce, adding 2 tablespoons of vegetable oil to the mixture. This will prevent the skin from getting dried out. You might also add a loose foil cover at this time to keep the skin from getting too dark. Decrease the oven heat to 375 degrees and continue to bake for another 30 minutes. To test for doneness, cut into the thickest part of the chicken; it should not be pink.

TURKEY WITH OYSTER DRESSING

Everyone seems to have a best way to cook a turkey.
I've experimented with everything from precooking
and reheating to baking it in one of my husband's
green Marine skivvy shirts. Currently I cook it loosely
covered in foil until the final browning, and baste it
frequently. My oyster dressing is very simple: for an
average-sized turkey, say 10 to 12 pounds, I use 2
10-ounce jars of oysters. (These are fresh West Coast
oysters.) Cut them up if they're large, saving the juice.
Add about 6 cups of cubed, slightly stale French bread,
2 cups of minced celery, 1 cup of minced onion, and 1
melted stick of margarine, and mix all the ingredients
together with the oyster juice. Stuff the turkey and
secure it firmly. Rub the outside of the bird wih a
mixture of safflower oil and margarine.

TURKEY WITH TUNA

(Start the day before)

1 6-pound turkey breast, thawed	½ teaspoon thyme
	1 tube anchovy paste
1 large onion, chopped	Capers
2 stalks celery, chopped	3 cups safflower oil mayonnaise
2 cloves garlic, crushed	
1 carrot, chopped	2 cups converted rice
1 8-ounce can solid pack white tuna (in oil)	3 tablespoons safflower oil
9 cups chicken broth	1 cup parsley, finely chopped
1 cup white wine	

Remove any fat from the turkey breast, and place
breast down in a large heavy pan that has a cover.
Add all the other ingredients except the last five. There
should be enough liquid to cover the meat; if not add
more broth or water. Bring to a boil, reduce heat,
cover pan with wax paper and lid, and simmer till

turkey is tender—about two hours. Place covered pan in refrigerator over night.

The following day remove the breast, wrap it in foil and return to refrigerator. Over high heat reduce the liquid to about four cups; strain through a fine sieve. Refrigerate. When cold, skim off fat from top. Put the mayonnaise in a bowl and gradually beat in enough of the broth to make a thick smooth sauce. Carve the turkey in thin uniform slices. Cook 2 cups of converted rice; when done add 3 tablespoons safflower oil, then 1 cup finely chopped parsley. Mound on a large platter, and arrange the turkey slices down the center of the rice. Mask the meat with the sauce; it should be just of a consistency to coat the slices. Garnish with capers. Serve the remaining sauce in a bowl.

The leftovers from this disk will make a great dinner for the next night. You'll have some of the sauce left, as there is quite a lot. Cook some spaghetti, cut the remaining turkey into small pieces and add to the hot sauce. Pour over spaghetti and serve.

24

Vegetables

CREAMED CABBAGE

Pour boiling water over a small head of shredded cabbage and allow to cook for 3 minutes. Drain the cabbage, hold it under cold running water, and again drain it. Sauté 3 tablespoons of minced onion in 1 tablespoon of margarine until soft, add the cabbage, ¼ cup of safflower mayonnaise, ¼ teaspoon of dill weed, and salt to taste. Simmer, stirring and tossing, for about 3 minutes.

GADO GADO

A Dutch friend of mine serves this delicious Indonnesian vegetable dish for lunch. The combination of ingredients is such that one need serve nothing else; it's a complete meal.

Cut up and steam 4 or 5 vegetables such as carrots, bean sprouts, brussels sprouts, green beans, and cabbage. (The bean sprouts are a must.) They should be crisply undercooked. Arrange them in neat sections in a serving dish and allow them to cool to room temperature. Make a sauce of peanut butter —the crunchy kind—and water. It should be about the consistency of mayonnaise. Put it on the stove and stir till smooth, then add a crushed clove of garlic, a little cayenne (just a dash), soy sauce to taste, and some finely minced onion. Serve the sauce luke-warm in a separate bowl with the cooked vegetables; you'll find tastes will vary as to the amount of sauce desired. Shrimp-flavored chips, *koepoek,* available in many grocery stores, are delicious served with this dish.

POLENTA

2 cups water
½ cup cornmeal

2 tablespoons margarine

Bring the water to a boil, slowly add the cornmeal, and boil for 5 minutes. Add the margarine, place in a baking dish, and bake for about 30 minutes in a 350-degree oven.

DOLLAR POTATOES

Choose long, not round, baking potatoes. Holding the potato firmly in one hand, slice it thinly across the narrow way so that you have a series of slices about the size of silver dollars. Keeping the potato slices to-gether so the potato is in its original shape, place in a pan where it will fit snugly and not fall apart. (If necessary, pad around it with foil.) Brush well with margarine and bake 1 hour at 400 degrees, or until crisp and done.

RICE PILAF WITH VEGETABLES

½ cup margarine
1 cup diced, peeled eggplant
1 small zucchini, diced
2 large mushrooms, sliced
1 clove garlic, crushed

1 small can pimentos, minced
1 teaspoon salt
1 cup rice
2 cups chicken broth

Melt ½ cup of margarine in a saucepan, add everything except the rice and broth, and sauté lightly. Add
the broth, bring to a boil, add the rice. Cover tightly
and cook over low heat for about 30 minutes.

CREAMED SPINACH

1 package frozen chopped   Pinch nutmeg
  spinach   Dash salt
¼ cup safflower mayon-
  naise

This is one of the few times I use a frozen vegetable
for convenience. (The spinach is all chopped and
easy to use, but you may very well prefer to cook and
chop fresh spinach.) Without adding any water, cook
the spinach in a covered pan only till defrosted and
very hot. Gradually stir in the mayonnaise over very
low heat. Add a pinch of nutmeg, a dash of salt, stir
till very hot and smooth, and serve at once.

SPINACH-STUFFED MUSHROOM CAPS

½ package frozen spinach   Salt to taste
1 tablespoon margarine   4 large mushrooms, washed
1 tablespoon flour   and peeled (if necessary)
Pinch nutmeg

Cook the spinach slightly, saving the juice. Melt the
margarine and add the flour, stirring to make a roux.
Gradually add enough spinach water to make a thick
sauce, about ½ cup. Add the nutmeg, salt to taste,
then mix with the spinach. Stuff the mushroom cups
and cook in a 350-degree oven till the mushrooms are
done—around 7 to 10 minutes.

VEGETABLE TACOS

Sliced fresh mushrooms
Chopped green onions
Chopped green peppers
Alfalfa sprouts
Corn tortillas

1 very ripe avocado, peeled
    and mashed
1 clove garlic, crushed
1 tablespoon very finely
    chopped onion
1 drop Tabasco sauce

Sauté the mushrooms or serve them raw, as desired. Arrange the vegetables on a platter, heat the tortillas, and made a guacamole out of the mashed avocado, garlic, finely chopped onion, and drop of Tabasco. Rice may be added to this spread if a heartier taco is wished. You make your own tacos by placing the vegetables on the tortillas, adding guacamole, and rolling them up to eat with your fingers.

VEGETABLES WITH HERBS

2 slices eggplant
1 small zucchini
1 green pepper
1 small onion
Olive oil
Safflower oil
French bread crumbs

2 tablespoons chopped
    parsley
1 clove garlic, crushed
½ teaspoon crumbled basil
Large pinch each, rosemary
    and sage
¼ teaspoon salt

Slice the vegetables and moisten them with olive and safflower oil, mixed. Lay them in a baking pan and top with French bread crumbs mixed with 2 tablespoons of chopped parsley, 1 clove of garlic, crushed, ½ teaspoon of crumbled basil, a large pinch each of rosemary and sage, and ¼ teaspoon of salt. Bake in a 350-degree oven till crisply tender. Allow to cool before serving.

BRAISED ZUCCHINI

Slice the zucchini on the diagonal, about ½ inch thick, and place in a heavy pan with a pat of margarine. Melt the margarine, add salt, and cover. Braise over very low heat till tender but not soft—no more than 10 minutes should be enough.

ZUCCHINI FRITATTA

3 or 4 zucchini, chopped	3 egg whites, beaten
1 smallish onion, chopped	2 tablespoons flour
1 clove garlic, crushed	Salt
2 tablespoons olive oil	Dash nutmeg

Sauté the vegetables and garlic in the olive oil lightly. Beat the egg whites just until frothy; add the flour, salt, and nutmeg. Mix with the vegetables and pour into a small, shallow baking dish. Bake just until the eggs are set—about 8 minutes in a 350-degree oven.

25

Desserts

DR. DONG'S BASIC RICE PUDDING

11 cups water   2 cups uncooked rice

Thoroughly wash the rice until the water runs clear.
This is very important! Put the rice in a blender and
add about 1 cup of cold water. Blend on the medium
and then on the highest speed four times. The mixture
will be milky and pulverized. Meanwhile, bring 10 cups
of water to a rapid boil in a heavy container. Add the
contents of the blender *very slowly*, stirring constantly
with a serrated spoon. It will thicken almost immediately. Don't be afraid of this consistency; it will
smooth out during the boiling. Boil about 25 minutes,
stirring occasionally, and if the mixture seems too
lumpy use your eggbeater a few times while cooking.
Pour into a bowl and chill. This mixture may be used
as a cereal, a thickening agent for soups, with tuna, or
as a dessert pudding with the addition of brown sugar
or honey. The pudding will keep well covered, in the
refrigerator.

PECAN DESSERT

¾ cup sugar   4 egg whites, beaten
1¼ cups light corn syrup   1½ cups pecans or walnuts
½ cup margarine, melted   Coconut cream (canned)
1 teaspoon vanilla

Beat the sugar, corn syrup, margarine, and vanilla together; add the beaten egg whites and nuts and turn into an oiled 8-inch-square baking pan. Bake in a 375-degree oven 35 to 40 minutes. Spoon into dessert dishes. Serve with a pitcher of coconut cream.

VANILLA SOUFFLÉ

4 tablespoons margarine	¼ teaspoon almond extract
4 tablespoons flour	4 egg whites, stiffly beaten
1 cup water	Powdered sugar
⅓ cup superfine sugar	⅓ cup toasted chopped
1 teaspoon vanilla	almonds

Make a white sauce of the margarine, flour, and water; stir in the sugar and flavorings. Fold in the stiffly beaten egg whites, turn into an oiled soufflé dish, and sprinkle with the powdered sugar. Place in a pan of hot water and bake in a 350-degree oven for about 55 minutes, or till firm. Sprinkle with the almonds and serve immediately.

ANGEL CREAM

5 egg whites, stiffly beaten	1 teaspoon vanilla
¾ cup superfine sugar	¾ cup grated almonds

Beat the egg whites till stiff, add ½ cup of the sugar, and then gently fold in the remaining ¼ cup. Add the vanilla and gently fold in the almonds (these can be grated in a blender). Angel Cream should be served very cold, so since it must be done at the last minute (or the egg whites will separate), I keep the ingredients in the refrigerator until ready to make it. It only takes a few minutes to do so, and it is delicious served in your best sherbet glasses.

SABAYON

1 package unflavored gelatin	Pinch salt
½ cup cold water	¾ cup cold water
3 tablespoons sugar	3 tablespoons Marsala wine
	2 egg whites

Melt the gelatin in the ½ cup cold water, place over low heat and stir for about three minutes. Remove from heat and stir in the sugar, salt, water, and wine. Chill until the mixture is slightly thickened. Beat egg whites until stiff, then as you add the sugar mixture continue beating until it becomes very light, frothy, and has doubled in volume. Chill until set.

PUMPKIN CHIFFON PIE

Crust:

1½ cups finely ground Brazil nuts	3 tablespoons sugar

Filling:

1 tablespoon unflavored gelatin	1 teaspoon cinnamon
¼ cup cold water	½ teaspoon ginger
1½ cups cooked pumpkin	½ cup water
½ cup sugar	2 egg whites, stiffly beaten
1¼ teaspoons salt	¼ cup shredded, toasted Brazil nuts

Combine the 1½ cups of nuts with the 3 tablespoons of sugar and line an 8-inch pie plate. Soften the gelatin in ¼ cup of cold water. Combine the pumpkin, ¼ cup of the sugar, the salt, spices, and ½ cup of water; cook over boiling water for 5 minutes, stirring constantly. Add the softened gelatin and stir until the gelatin is dissolved. Chill until slightly thickened. Then gradually beat the remaining ¼ cup of sugar into the stiffly beaten egg whites and fold into the thickened pumpkin-gelatin mixture. Pour the filling on the crust mixture in the pie plate and top with the shredded nuts. Chill until firm.

ANGEL FOOD CAKE

1½ cups sugar	1 teaspoon almond extract
4 tablespoons water	1 cup cake flour
1 cup egg whites, stiffly beaten	¼ teaspoon salt
	1 teaspoon cream of tartar

Boil the sugar and water together until a thread forms when a spoon is dipped into it. Beat the egg whites until stiff; gradually beat in the sugar mixture, then add the almond extract and beat until cooled. Mix and sift the flour and other dry ingredients several times; then gradually fold in the beaten egg-white mixture. Bake in an ungreased angel-food tin at 275 degrees for 30 minutes, then at 375 degrees until the cake springs back when pressed with a finger—about 7 to 10 minutes.

CARROT CAKE

1 cup margarine, softened	⅔ cup finely chopped toasted walnuts
2 cups sugar	2½ cups sifted all-purpose flour
4 egg whites	3 teaspoons baking powder
1 teaspoon ground cinnamon	½ teaspoon salt
½ teaspoon nutmeg	⅓ cup warm water
1½ cups finely grated carrots	

Beat the soft margarine and sugar until light and fluffy, then beat in the egg whites and spices. Stir in the carrots and nuts. Sift the dry ingredients and add to the mixture alternately with the water. (Do not beat the flour mixture in, but rather fold it in till it is moistened.) Turn into an oiled and floured 11x15-inch pan, and bake in a preheated 350-degree oven for 35 minutes or until the cake springs back when pressed lightly in the center. Cool on a cake rack.

MAYONNAISE CAKE

1 teaspoon baking soda
½ cup chopped walnuts
½ cup chopped almonds
1 cup boiling water

1 cup sugar
1¾ cups flour
1 teaspoon cinnamon
1 cup safflower mayonnaise

Add the soda to the nuts and pour the boiling water over them. Let cool. Mix the sugar, flour, and cinnamon with the mayonnaise, combine with the nuts, and bake in a 9x9-inch pan for about 30 minutes at 350 degrees.

ALMOND OATMEAL COOKIES

1½ sticks margarine
1 cup brown sugar
¼ cup water
1 generous teaspoon almond flavoring

1 cup flour
½ teaspoon baking soda
1 teaspoon salt
2 cups Quick Quaker Oats
½ cup finely chopped blanched almonds

Mix the margarine, sugar, water, and almond flavoring and beat till smooth. Sift the dry ingredients together and add to the creamy mixture. Add the Quaker Oats and almonds. Drop by the teaspoonful onto greased cookie sheets and press down slightly. Bake for 14 minutes at 350 degrees.

ITALIAN ANISE COOKIES

3 cups sifted unbleached flour
1 cup sugar
1 tablespoon baking powder
1½ teaspoons salt

4 egg whites
2 to 3 teaspoons crushed anise seeds
1 cup chopped roasted almonds

Sift the flour with the sugar, baking powder, and salt. Beat the egg whites slightly with a fork; mix in the anise seeds and flour mixture to make a soft dough. Divide in half. Roll each half into a 10x8-inch rectangle. Sprinkle with the almonds and roll up as for a jelly roll, starting from the 10-inch side. Slide onto a greased cookie sheet and flatten to about 1 inch in height. Bake at 350 degrees for 20 to 25 minutes or until lightly browned. Cool slightly and slice into ½ inch pieces; return the slices to the cookie sheet and toast in a 350-degree oven for 4 or 5 minutes.

MACAROONS

6 egg whites
½ teaspoon salt
1 cup sugar
6 or 7 ounces blanched
   almonds

¼ cup white cornmeal or
   matzo meal
½ teaspoon rum flavoring

Beat the egg whites and salt until fairly stiff; then add the sugar slowly, continuing to beat until the egg whites form firm peaks. Grind the almonds in a blender until very fine and fork into the egg whites. Add the cornmeal and rum flavoring and drop the mixture by teaspoons onto an oiled cookie sheet. Flatten slightly with a spoon and bake in a 350-degree oven for about 20 minutes. Cool slightly before removing from the sheet; cool further on a rack.

PFEFFER NUTS

1 cup unblanched almonds
2 cups unsifted flour
1 teaspoon baking soda
¼ cup dark corn syrup
1 stick margarine
½ cup sugar

1½ teaspoons cinnamon
½ teaspoon nutmeg
¼ teaspoon cloves
¼ teaspoon salt
1 egg white
Powdered sugar

Grind the almonds coarsely in a blender; mix with the unsifted flour and baking soda. Combine all the rest of the ingredients except the egg white and powdered sugar in a saucepan and heat, stirring, until the margarine melts. Cool slightly, mix in the egg white, and gradually beat in the almond mixture. Chill the dough if it is too soft to handle, then shape it into balls about the size of walnuts. Bake the balls on an ungreased cookie sheet in a 375-degree oven for 15 to 20 minutes, checking to make sure they don't get too brown on the bottom. Shake the warm cookies, a few at a time, in a bag of powdered sugar.

SESAME SEED COOKIES

½ cup shredded coconut	½ teaspoon baking soda
1 cup sesame seeds	1 teaspoon baking powder
¾ cup corn oil	½ teaspoon salt
1 cup brown sugar	Vanilla or almond extract
2 cups flour	(whichever you prefer)

Spread the coconut and sesame seeds on a baking sheet and toast them lightly. Cream the oil and sugar and gradually sift in the dry ingredients. Add the vanilla or almond extract, and mix in the coconut and sesame seeds. Drop by the teaspoonful onto an oiled cookie sheet and bake for 12 minutes at 350 degrees.

Selected Bibliography for the Medical Section

Books

ABERCROMBIE, M., C. J. HICKMAN, AND M. L. JOHNSON. *A Dictionary of Biology*. Penguin Books, Baltimore, 1964.

ADAMS, JOHN CRAWFORD. *Arthritis and Back Pain*. University Park Press, Baltimore, 1972.

ANATOMICAL SCIENCES TRAINING COMMITTEE OF THE NATIONAL INSTITUTE OF GENERAL MEDICAL SCIENCES. *Cellular Aspects of Immune Reaction*. National Institutes of Health, Bethesda, Md., 1967.

ASCHNER, BERNARD, M.D. *Arthritis Can Be Cured*. The Julian Press, Inc., New York, 1957.

BARNES, C. G., et al. (editors). *Clinical Rheumatology*. J. B. Lippincott Co., Philadelphia, 1970.

BEACH, FRANK A. *Hormones and Behavior*. Paul B. Hoeber, Inc., New York, 1948.

BEECHER, HENRY K. *Measurement of Subjective Responses: Quantitative Effects of Drugs*. Oxford University Press, New York, 1959.

BICKNELL, FRANKLIN, AND FREDERICK PRESCOTT. *The American and His Food*. University of Chicago Press, Chicago, 1941.

BLAND, JOHN H., M.D. *Arthritis Medical Treatment and Home Care* (6th edition). Macmillan Company, New York, 1972.

BLAU, SHELDON PAUL, M.D., AND DODI SCHULTZ. *Arthritis: Complete, Up-to-Date Facts for Patients and Their*

Families. Doubleday and Co., Inc., Garden City, N.Y., 1974.

BODANSKY, M., AND O. BODANSKY. *Biochemistry of Disease* (2nd edition). Macmillan Company, New York, 1952.

BONICA, JOHN J. *The Management of Pain.* Lea & Febiger, Philadelphia, 1954.

BRIDGES, M. A. *Dietetics for the Clinician.* Lea & Febiger, Philadelphia, 1936.

BROOKE, JAMES W. *Arthritis and You.* Harper, New York, 1960.

BRUCH, DR. HILDE. *Eating Disorders: Obesity, and Anorexia Nervosa and the Person Within.* Basic Books, New York, 1973.

BURNETT, SIR MCFARLANE. *Natural History of Infectious Disease* (4th edition). Cambridge University Press, New York, 1972.

CALABRO, JOHN J., M.D., AND JOHN WYKERT. *The Truth About Arthritis Care.* David McKay Co., Inc., New York, 1971.

CLARK, STANLEY K., M.D., C.M., F.R.C.P. *What to Eat—and When* (9th edition). Pantagraph Press, Ltd., Bloomington, Ill., 1971.

COLLINS, W. DOUGLAS, M.D. *Illustrated Manual of Laboratory Diagnosis: Indications and Interpretations.* J. B. Lippincott Co., Philadelphia, 1968.

COOPER, F. L., et al. *Nutrition in Health and Disease* (14th edition). J. B. Lippincott Co., Philadelphia, 1958.

DAVIDSON, SIR STANLEY, A. P. MIKLEJOHN, AND R. PASSMORE. *Human Nutrition and Dietetics.* Williams and Wilkins Co., Baltimore, 1959.

DOWNING, JOHN GODWIN. *The Cutaneous Manifestations of Systemic Diseases.* Charles C. Thomas, Publisher, Springfield, Ill., 1954.

DUNBAR, ROBERT E., AND SEGALL, HOWARD F. *A Doctor Discusses Learning to Cope with Arthritis, Rheumatism, and Gout.* Budlong, Chicago, 1973.

ENGLE, GEORGE L. *Psychological Development in Health and Disease.* W. B. Saunders Co., Philadelphia, 1962.

EWART, CHARLES. *The Healing Needles: A Story of Acupuncture and Its Pioneer Practitioner, Dr. Louis Moss.* Elm Tree Books, Hamish Hamilton, London, 1972.

FIELD, HAZEL E. *Foods in Health and Disease.* Macmillan Company, New York, 1964.

FLATT, ADRIANEDE. *The Care of the Rheumatoid Hand.* Mosby, St. Louis, 1974.

FOOD AND NUTRITION BOARD. *Recommended Dietary Allowances* (7th edition). National Academy of Sciences, Washington, D.C., 1968.

FRIEDENWALD, J., AND J. RUHRA. *Diet in Health and Disease.* W. B. Saunders Co., Philadelphia, 1925.

GOFMAN, JOHN W., PH.D., M.D., ALEX V. NICHOLS, PH.D., AND E. VIRGINIA DOBBIN. *Dietary Prevention and Treatment of Heart Disease.* G. P. Putnam's Sons, New York, 1958.

GOLDING, DOUGLAS M. *A Synopsis of Rheumatic Diseases.* Williams and Wilkins Co., Baltimore, 1973.

GOOD, ROBERT A., AND DAVID W. FISHER (editors). *Immunobiology.* Sinauer Associates, Inc., Stamford, Conn., 1971.

HARRIS, M. COLEMAN, M.D., AND NORMAN SHURE, M.D. *All About Allergy.* Prentice-Hall, Inc., Englewood Cliffs, N.J., 1969.

HAWKINS, HAROLD F. *Applied Nutrition.* Institute Press, Gardena, Calif., 1940.

HEYNINGEN, W. E. VAN. *Bacterial Toxins.* Charles C. Thomas, Publisher, Springfield, Ill., 1959.

HOLLANDER, JOSEPH LEE, M.D. *Arthritis and Allied Conditions: A Textbook of Rheumatology* (7th edition). Lea & Febiger, Philadelphia, 1956.

HORROBIN, DAVID F. *The Communication System of the Body.* Basic Books, New York, 1964.

HUEPER, W. C., AND W. D. CONWAY. *Chemical Carcinogenesis and Cancers.* Charles C. Thomas, Publisher, Springfield, Ill., 1965.

JAYSON, MALCOLM I. V., M.D., AND ALAN ST. J. DIXON, M.D. *Understanding Arthritis and Rheumatism: A Complete Guide to the Problems and Treatment.* Pantheon Books, New York, 1974.

KEATS, ARTHUR S. *New Concepts in Pain and Its Clinical Management.* F. A. Davis Co., Philadelphia, 1967.

LAKESIDE LABORATORIES. *Metabolic Individuality and Diagnosis of Degenerative Disease.* Milwaukee, 1951.

LAMB, MINA W., AND MARGARETTE L. HARDEN. *The Meaning of Human Nutrition.* Pergamon Press, Inc., Elmsford, N.Y., 1973.

LEONARD, JON N., JACK L. HOFER, AND NATHAN PRITIKIN. *Live Longer Now: The First One Hundred Years of*

Your Life: The 2100 Program. Grosset & Dunlap, Inc., New York, 1974.

LEVI, LENNART (editor). *Society, Stress and Disease.* Vol. I, *The Psychosocial Environment and Psychosomatic Diseases.* Oxford University Press, New York, 1971.

LEWIS, FAYE C. *All Out Against Arthritis.* Prentice-Hall, Inc., Englewood Cliffs, N.J., 1973.

LIEFMANN, DR. ROBERT E. *Arthritis Discovery.* Commonwealth Publishing Co., Freeport, Bahamas, 1971.

MCCARRISON, SIR ROBERT, AND H. M. SINCLAIR. *Nutrition and Health.* Faber and Faber, London, 1953.

MCCOLLUM, E. V., AND J. ERNESTINE BECKER, *Food, Nutrition, and Health.* (3rd edition). Baltimore, 1934.

MCCOLLUM, E. V., AND N. SIMMONDS. *The Newer Knowledge of Nutrition.* Macmillan Company, New York, 1929.

MCDEVITT, HUGH O., AND MAURICE LANDY (editors). *Genetic Control of Immune Responsiveness.* Academic Press, New York, 1972.

MCLESTER, J. S. *Nutrition and Diet in Health and Disease.* W. B. Saunders Co., Philadelphia, 1927.

MANN, FELIX, M.D. *Acupuncture: The Ancient Chinese Art of Healing and How It Works Scientifically.* Vintage Books, New York, 1971.

MANN, FELIX, M.D. *The Treatment of Disease by Acupuncture.* William Heinemann Medical Books, Ltd., London, 1972.

Medical Illustrations of Common Joint Diseases. Eli Lilly & Co., Indianapolis, 1968.

MONIER-WILLIAMS, G. W. *Trace Elements in Food.* John Wiley & Sons, New York, 1949.

PAGE, IRVINE, M.D. *Speaking to the Doctor: His Responsibilities and Opportunities.* Proforum, Minneapolis, 1972.

PRICE, WESTON A. *Nutrition and Physical Degeneration.* American Academy of Applied Nutrition, Los Angeles, 1939.

QUIGLEY, D. T. *The National Malnutrition.* Lee Foundation for Nutritional Research, Milwaukee, 1943.

RAGEN, CHARLES, AND ARTHUR I. SNYDER. *Rheumatoid Arthritis.* Yearbook Publishers, Chicago, 1955.

RAPAPORT, HOWARD G., M.D., AND SHIRLEY MOTTER LINDE, M.S. *The Complete Allergy Guide.* Simon & Schuster, Inc., New York, 1970.

RICHARDS, VICTOR. *Cancer: The Wayward Cell.* University of California Press, Berkeley, 1972.

ROSE, MARY SWARTZ. *The Foundations of Nutrition.* Macmillan Company, New York, 1933.

ROWE, ALBERT H., M.D. *Food Allergy.* Lea & Febiger, Philadelphia, 1931.

SHERMAN, H. C. *Chemistry of Food and Nutrition.* Macmillan Company, New York, 1932.

SCHMECK, HAROLD M. *Immunology: The Many-Edged Sword.* George Braziller, Inc., New York, 1974.

SMITH, RICHARD T., AND MAURICE LANDY (editors). *Immune Surveillance.* Academic Press, New York, 1970.

STERN, FRANCES. *Applied Dietetics.* Williams and Wilkins Co., Baltimore, 1943.

TAN, LEONG T., MARGARET Y.-C. TAN, AND ILZA VEITH, M.D. *Acupuncture Therapy: Current Chinese Practice.* Temple University Press, Philadelphia, 1973.

TAUBE, E. LOUIS, M.D. *Food Allergy and the Allergic Patient: A Simple Review of Problems Encountered by the Recently Diagnosed Patient.* Charles C. Thomas, Publisher, Springfield, Ill., 1973.

TURNER, JAMES S. (project director). *The Chemical Feast.* Ralph Nader Study Group Report on Food Protection and Food and Drug Administration, Grossman Publishers, Inc., New York, 1970.

WILLIAMS, ROGER. *Alcoholism: The Nutritional Approach.* University of Texas Press, Austin, 1959.

WILLIAMS, ROGER I. *Nutrition Against Disease: Environmental Prevention.* Pitman Publishing Co., New York, 1971.

WILLIAMS, SUE RODWELL. *Nutrition and Diet Therapy* (2nd edition). C. B. Mosby & Co., St. Louis, 1973.

WILSON, DAVID. *Body and Antibody: A Report on the New Immunology.* Alfred A. Knopf Co., Inc., New York, 1971.

WINTON, ANDREW LINCOLN, AND K. G. WINTON. *Structure and Composition of Foods* (2 volumes). John Wiley & Sons, 1935.

WOHL, M. G., AND R. S. GOODHART (editors). *Modern Nutrition in Health and Disease.* Lea & Febiger, Philadelphia, 1960.

WOLFF, HAROLD G. *Stress and Disease.* Charles C. Thomas, Publisher, Springfield, Ill., 1953.

WOLFF, STEWART, AND HAROLD G. WOLFF. *Headaches: Their Nature and Treatment*. Little, Brown, Boston, 1953.

Periodicals

AMMANN, ARTHUR J., M.D. "How to Use Autoimmune Tests in Your Practice," *Consultant*, March 1975, Vol. 15, No. 3, P. 55.

"Ankylosing Spondylitis Seems to Be Hereditary," *JAMA**, Aug. 19, 1974, Vol. 229, No. 8, pp. 1035–6.

AREES, EDWARD A., AND JEAN MAYER. "Monosodium Glutamate-Induced Brain Lesions: Electron Microscopic Examination," *Science*, Oct. 30, 1970, p. 549–550.

"Arthritis and Drug Abuse," *Medical Times*, September 1974, Vol. 102, No. 9, p. 103–4.

AXLEROD, A. "Nutrition in Relation to Acquired Immunity," *Modern Nutrition in Health and Disease*, 1973.

BASKIND, MORTON S. "The Technique of Nutritional Therapy," *Journal of Applied Nutrition*, 1960, Vol. 13, No. 1.

BONICA, J. J., M.D. "Acupuncture Anesthesia in the People's Republic of China," *JAMA*, Sept. 2, 1974, Vol. 229, No. 10, p. 1317.

BORTZ, E. L. "Mechanisms of Aging," *Journal of the American Geriatrics Society*, 1959, Vol. 7, p. 825.

BROOKS, CARTER D., M.D., et al. "Tolerance and Pharmacology of Ibuprofen," *Current Therapeutic Research*, April 1973, Vol. 15, No. 4, pp. 180–190.

BRYAN, WILLIAM J., JR., M.D., J.D., PH.D., L.L.D., F.A.I.H., F.A.C.M. "The Law of Acupuncture," *Journal of the American Institute of Hypnosis*, November 1973, Vol. 14, No. 6.

BUTTERWORTH, CHARLES E., JR., M.D. "The Skeleton in the Hospital Closet," *Nutrition Today*, March/April 1974.

CANNON, P. "The Importance of Proteins in Resistance to Infection," *JAMA*, 1945, Vol. 128, p. 360.

CLAUSEN, S. W. "The Influence of Nutrition upon Resistance to Infection," *Physiological Review*, 1934, Vol. 14, p. 309.

_____
* Journal of the American Medical Association.

CROW, DR. JAMES. "Do Chemicals Sow the Seeds of Genetic Change?" *Medical World News,* Apr. 26, 1968.

DALESSIO, D. J., M.D. "Dietary Allergy in Vascular Headaches," *JAMA,* Apr. 28, 1975, Vol. 232, No. 4, p. 400.

"Dietary Fibre and Disease," *JAMA,* Aug. 19, 1974, Vol. 229, No. 8, p. 1068.

"Does Human Antibiotic Resistance Relate to Feed Supplements?" *Infectious Diseases,* December 1974, p. 3.

DOLE, V. P., et al. "Dietary Treatment of Hypertension," *Journal of Clinical Investigation,* 1951, Vol. 30, p. 1189.

EHRLICH, GEORGE E., M.D., "Easing Pain Stiffness of Arthritis Outline," *Chronic Disease,* October 1974.

FARRAR, J. T., M.D. "There Is Too Much Stress On Bland Diet," *Medical Opinion,* September 1974, pp. 31–36.

"Food Additives: Health Question Awaiting an Answer," *Medical World News,* September 7, 1973, Vol. 14, No. 32, p. 72.

FRAZIER, CLAUDE E., M.D. "Introduction to Allergy," *Medical Insight,* June 1973, pp. 12–17.

"Gold Therapy in Rheumatoid Arthritis," *Annals of Rheumatic Disease,* 1960, Vol. 19, p. 95.

"Gold Therapy in Rheumatoid Arthritis: Improving the Results," *Consultant,* November 1974, pp. 95–97.

GOLDING, D. N., M.D., F.R.C.P.I. "Problems in Rheumatology: Non-Articular Arthritis," *Update International,* April 1974.

GOLDING, D. N., M.D., F.R.C.P.I. "Variants in Rheumatology," *Update International,* June 1974.

GRACE, LINDA. "There Are No Harmless Substances," *World Health,* April 1969, pp. 20–22.

HAGY AND SETTIPANE. "Bronchial Asthma, Allergic Rhinitis and Allergy Skin Test Among College Students," *Journal of Allergy,* December 1969, Vol. 44, No. 6.

HUANG, S., AND T. M. BAYLESS. "Milk and Lactose Intolerance in Healthy Orientals," *Science,* 1968, Vol. 160, pp. 83–84.

HURSH, L. M., M.D. "Milk Has Something for Everybody?" *JAMA,* May 5, 1975, Vol. 232, No. 5.

JAMES, LYNNE, PH.D. "Diet-Related Birth Defects," *Nutrition Today,* July/August 1974, p. 4.

JOHNSON, PAUL E. "Health Aspects of Food Additives," *American Journal of Public Health,* June 1966, Vol. 56, No. 6.

"Joint Pain: Is It Really Rheumatoid Arthritis?" *Patient Care,* May 1, 1974, p. 27.

JUKES, THOMAS H., PH.D., D.Sc. "The Organic Food Myth," *JAMA,* Oct, 14, 1974, Vol. 230, No. 2, p. 276.

KEYS, A., et al. "Lessons From Serum Cholesterol Studies In Japan, Hawaii and Los Angeles," *Annals of Internal Medicine,* 1958, Vol. 48, pp. 83–94.

KHAIRI, M. RASHIDA, M.D., et al. "Treatment of Paget Disease of the Bone (Osteitis Deformans): Results of a One-Year Study with Sodium Etidronate," *JAMA,* Oct. 28, 1974, Vol. 230, No. 4, p. 562–7.

KLINGER, ALFRED D., M.D. "Confronting Our Inadequate Nutrition," *Medical Tribune,* Aug. 14, 1974, p. 6.

LEVIN, MELVIN H., M.D. "Gout: The Many Facets of Therapy," *Consultant,* January 1974, pp. 27–29.

LITCHFIELD, JOHN T., JR., M.D. "Drug Toxicity in the Human Fetus and Newborn," *Applied Therapeutics,* September 1967, pp. 922–926.

LOONEY, GERALD L., M.D. "Acupuncture Vindication May Lie in Basic Research," *Modern Medicine,* April 1975, p. 128.

"Low Synovial Fluid Complement Linked to More Disabling Arthritis," *Geriatrics,* March 1975, p. 193.

MACLAREN, WALTER R., M.D., F.A.C.A., et. al. "The Rat Masked Cell Degranulation Test As Applied to a Case of Severe Food Allergy," *Annals of Allergy,* January 1972, Vol. 30, pp. 41–44.

"Major Breakthrough Against Arthritis," *National Tattler,* Sept. 29, 1974, Vol. 21, No. 13.

MALTZ, BERTRAM A., M.D. "Guide to Arthritis Diagnosis," *Chronic Disease,* May 1974.

MAYER, DR. JEAN. "What Every Doctor Should Know About Foods," *Physician's World,* October 1974, Vol. 2, No. 10, p. 50.

MELNICK, ARNOLD, D.O. "Helping the Child with Juvenile Rheumatoid Arthritis," *Medical Opinion,* August 1974, p. 76.

MERKIN, CARL. "Diet the Key to Controlling Arthritis," *Prevention,* July 1974, pp. 134–143.

MICHELMORE, PETER. "A Model Geriatric Health Care System: Coordinated Endeavor of Patient Care and Physician Training," *Geriatrics,* February 1975, p. 146.

MORRISON, L. M. "Diet in Coronary Arteriosclerosis," *JAMA*, 1960, Vol. 173, pp. 884–888.

NELSON, JERE J., M.D. "Relieving Select Symptoms of the Elderly," *Geriatrics*, March 1975, Vol. 30, No. 3, p. 113.

"New Drugs May Soon Supplement Aspirin in Treating Arthritics," *Medical News*, July 29, 1974, pp. 505–508.

"New Tests of Diet Urged as Coronary Disease Curb," *Chronic Disease*, December 1974, Vol. 8, No. 12.

"The Nutrition Factor: Its Role in National Development," *Nutrition Today*, November/December 1973, Vol. 8, No. 6.

"Nutritional Immunity: Host's Attempt to Withhold Iron from Microbial Invaders," *JAMA*, Jan. 6, 1975, Vol. 231, No. 1.

"Nutritional Immunity and Iron," *Infectious Diseases*, December 1974, p. 9.

PERLMAN, HENRY HARRIS, M.D. "The Formulary of Dermatologicals for Children," *Drug Therapy*, January 1975, pp. 85-96.

PETERMAN, R. A., AND R. S. GOODHART. "Current Status of Vitamin Therapy in Nervous and Mental Disease," *Journal of Clinical Nutrition*, 1954, Vol. 2, pp. 11–21.

PRESS, EDWARD, M.D., AND LEONA YEAGER, M.D. "Food Poisoning Due to Sodium Nicotinate," *American Journal of Public Health*, October 1962.

RAPP, DORIS J. M.D. "Milk Allergy from Birth to Old Age," *Consultant*, September 1974, pp. 120–122.

"The Relationship to Brain Development and Behavior," *Nutrition Today*, July/August 1974, p. 12.

"Removing Artificial Colors, Flavors Reported Beneficial in MBD," *Family Practice News*, Vol. 4, No. 13, p. 15.

RINZLER, S. H. "Prevention of Heart Disease by Diet," *Bulletin of the New York Academy of Medicine*, Vol. 44, pp. 936–949.

ROPES, M. W., et al. "Proposed Diagnostic Criteria for Rheumatoid Arthritis," *Bulletin of Rheumatic Diseases*, 1956, Vol. 7, p. 121.

RUDDY, SHAUN, AND HARVEY R. COLTEN. "Rheumatoid Arthritis: Biosynthesis of Complement Protein by Synovial Tissues," *The New England Journal of Medicine*, June 6, 1974, Vol. 290, No. 23, pp. 1284–1288.

RUDOLPH, CHARLES J., JR., PH.D. "Immunology and Nutrition," *Osteopathic Annals,* July 1974, pp. 45–50.

"Safe Use of Chemicals in Foods: Council Statement," *JAMA,* Nov. 18, 1961, Vol. 178, No. 7, p. 749.

SAMTER, MAX, M.D., AND RAY BEERS, JR., M.D. "Intolerance to Aspirin: Clinical Studies and Consideration of Its Pathogenesis," *Annals of Internal Medicine,* May 1968, Vol. 68, No. 5.

SANDERS, HOWARD J. "Food Additives" *Chemical and Engineering News,* 1966.

SILBERBERG, R., AND M. SILBERBERG. "Skeletal Growth and Articular Changes in Mice Receiving High-Fat Diet," *American Journal of Pathology,* 1950, Vol. 26, p. 113.

SKOSEY, JOHN L., M.D., PH.D. "Rheumatoid Arthritis: Overlooked, Underestimated, and Confusing," *Consultant,* July 1974, pp. 23–27.

TAO, GEORGE. "Chinese Food Therapy: High Blood Pressure and You." *China Medical Reporter,* March 1973, Vol. 1, No. 2.

"Treating Infectious Arthritis," *Infectious Diseases,* June 1974, p. 12.

"The Truth About Adverse Drug Reaction Deaths," *Viewpoint,* 1974, pp. 67–70.

TURPEINEN, et al. "Diet and Coronary Events," *Journal of the American Dietetics Association,* 1968, Vol. 52, pp. 209–213.

"Using Drugs in Elderly: Specialist Gives 7 Rules," *Chronic Disease,* March 1974, Vol. 8, No. 3, p. 2.

VINK, J. DE M., M.D. CH.B. "The Arthritis Patient and Family Practice," *Continuing Education for the Family Physician,* Vol. 3, No. 1, p. 2–31.

WATSON, GEORGE. "Note on Nutrition in Mental Illness," *Psychological Reports,* 1960, Vol. 6, No. 202.

WATSON, GEORGE, AND A. L. COMREY. "Nutritional Replacement for Mental Illness," *Journal of Psychology,* 1954, Vol. 38, pp. 251–264.

WEISS, HARVEY J., M.D. "Aspirin: A Dangerous Drug?" *JAMA,* Aug. 26, 1974, Vol. 229, No. 9.

"What Consumers Should Know About Food Additives," F.D.A. Publication No. 10, June 1962.

"White Whale Holds Hope for Antibody Studies of Human Autoimmune Disease," *Infectious Diseases,* June 1974, p. 17.

WICHER, KONRAD, ROBERT E. REISMAN, M.D., AND CARL E. ARBESMAN, M.D. "Allergic Reaction to Penicillin Present in Milk," *JAMA,* 1969, Vol. 208, No. 1, p. 143.

WITTIG, HEINZ J., M.D. "Diet for Children with Food Allergies," *Drug Therapy,* January 1975, pp. 129–141.

Also many publications of The Arthritis Foundation, the U.S. Department of Health, Education, and Welfare, and the National Institutes of Health.

Index

acids, 12, 13, 30, 132
acupuncture, 6, 112-124
  and electroacupuncture, 116-117
  fraudulent practitioners of, 117-118
  history of, 113, 117, 119
  techniques of, 116-117
  use of, in case histories, 10, 56, 59, 62, 124
additives, *see* chemical additives and preservatives
aging (*see also* gerontology, longevity), 103, 104
  in Far Eastern cultures, 105
  and mental senescence, 106, 108
Alabama, University of, Medical School, 34
alcohol, 20, 28-29, 41, 67, 68, 132
alfalfa sprouts, 133
alkaline secretions, 12, 13
Allergies—What They Are and What to Do About Them (Rudolph), 78
allergy, 74-94
  as cause of arthritis, 10, 36, 42, 79-80, 91
  to chemical additives, 29, 36, 47, 56, 77-78
  to chemicals in medicines, 10, 35
  and foods, 11, 36, 47, 56, 74, 76-78, 82
  history of food and, 74
  medical courses on, 76
  statistics on, 75-76
allopurinol, 42
almond oatmeal cookies, 215

amaranth (red No. 2), 31
American Board of Obstetrics and Gynecology, 6
American Congress of Cardiology, 26
American Heart Association, 26
  cookbook by, 26, 151
American Medical Association, 26, 102
American Public Health Association, 24
American Rheumatism Association, 38, 43, 86
amino acids, 13, 14, 144
amphetamines 77
amylase, 13
analgesics, 35, 118
Andes Mountains (Ecuador): longevity of population in, 105
anemia, 78
  iron deficiency, 53
angel cream, 212
angel food cake, 214
angioedema of the larynx, 78
anise cookies, Italian, 215-216
ankylosing spondylitis, 40
antibiotics, 104
antidepressants, 77
antimalarials, 51
antinuclear antibody test (ANA), 50
appendix, 13
appetizers, 176-177
  eggplant caviar, 176-177
  grape leaf rolls, 176
  herbed toast, 177
  shrimp pâté, 177
Apresolin, 67

229